85-1026

BEYOND THE AMERICAN HOUSING DREAM: ACCOMMODATION TO THE 1980s

Kenneth R. Tremblay, Jr.
University of Arkansas, Fayetteville

Don A. Dillman
Washington State University

WITHDRAWN

Shambaugh Library

UNIVERSITY
PRESS OF
AMERICA

LANHAM • NEW YORK • LONDON

Copyright © 1983 by

University Press of America,™ Inc.

4720 Boston Way
Lanham, MD 20706

3 Henrietta Street
London WC2E 8LU England

ISBN (Perfect): 0-8191-3479-1
ISBN   (Cloth): 0-8191-3478-3

All University Press of America books are produced on acid-free
paper which exceeds the minimum standards set by the National
Historical Publications and Records Commission.

to our parents,

for their love and support

iv

Contents

Preface

Where will Americans live in the late 1980s, the 1990s, and beyond? While owner-occupied detached single family houses may seem an obvious answer, there are several social dynamics which cast doubt on a continuation of this trend. Housing prices which are increasing faster than family incomes, high mortgage interest rates, changes in the availability of crucial building resources, and a concern over energy efficiency place the likelihood of most Americans owning detached single family homes in doubt.

This book examines future housing alternatives by reporting the results of a study on housing preferences. Housing preferences provide a gauge for measuring the kinds of homes in which people do and do not want to live. This study of 2,801 U.S. households reveals how Americans feel about living in a variety of housing environments, ranging from single family houses to mobile homes. Knowledge of people's housing preferences can then be utilized to understand where Americans will most likely live in the future, a crucial task.

It is hoped that our work will aid in the ultimate fulfillment of the often stated goal of a decent home and suitable living environment for every American family. Based upon recent housing trends, such a goal will be difficult to achieve in the future. However, knowledge of people's housing preferences can provide a starting point for the difficult housing decisions which lie ahead for policymakers and families.

There are several people who provided valuable support and encouragement for the writing of this book. Riley Dunlap and William Catton, Jr., both at Washington State University, provided important assistance during the course of this project. Harlowe Hatle, University of South Dakota, and Dorothy Larery, University of Arkansas, provided the time and encouragement to complete the writing of this book. Kent Van Liere, University of Tennessee, was a valuable resource person during the statistical analyses of the data. We also wish to thank Joye J. Dillman, Washington State University, for her vital role in the design and implementation of this project, and assistance with the interpretation of results. Our appreciation is also expressed to her for use of materials from publications which she co-authored. These and related publications from this project are listed in Appendix B.

viii

Our sincere thanks is also expressed to Louise Scott for her production assistance with the entire book. The assistance of Richard Rossi and Lela Odell is also gratefully acknowledged.

We are indebted to Washington State University for the institutional support that made possible the research upon which this book is based. The research was conducted under research project 0377 in the Home Economics Research Center and the Department of Rural Sociology, College of Agriculture, Washington State University, Pullman, Washington.

Finally, we must express thanks to the many individuals and families who gave freely of their time to participate in this study. Without them, this book would not have been possible.

Kenneth R. Tremblay, Jr.
Fayetteville, Arkansas

Don A. Dillman
Pullman, Washington

1

Housing in America

To live in a conventional single family detached house that one owns is more than an American Dream. For the majority of Americans, it is a firmly held life expectation as realistic as expecting to find a marriage partner, get a job, and have the right to vote. The thought of not being able to afford such a home is no less disconcerting than a constantly recurring nightmare.

Unfortunately, for an increasing number of Americans, hopes of buying their own conventionally built detached home may be a vanishing dream as they find themselves being priced out of their preferred housing market. The median-price of a new single family house is approaching $70,000, a price higher than a majority of Americans can afford based on traditional housing cost/family income formulas. To make matters worse, mortgage-interest rates are averaging about 13 to 14 percent, resulting in high monthly housing payments. Even if a family can raise the necessary money for a down payment and closing costs, it may face a rough road meeting monthly payments. It is estimated by some that three-fourths of American families cannot now afford the average priced home. The possibility of a young family with big dreams but little cash buying a conventional single family detached home is even more dismal.

Rising housing prices comprise only one side of the vise squeezing potential home buyers. The other side of the vise is a change in the availability of resources upon which housing is dependent. Energy to heat, cool, and power homes is in limited supply, a fact reflected in escalating energy bills for many Americans. Resources needed to provide adequate community services to homes, land on which to build, and certain building materials are being depleted at an uncomfortable pace. Some scholars question whether it is environmentally wise to provide conventional single family detached homes each on their own plot of land to people desiring them.

As a result of rising housing prices and changes in the availability of housing resources, ownership of a conventional single family detached house may indeed be a vanishing dream for many Americans. A substantial number of people will not be financially capable of purchasing conventional single family detached homes in the future. Even those able to afford their preferred housing environment may find that there exists an acute shortage of conventional single family detached homes for sale. Such a possibility comes at a time when a record number of Americans are searching for adequate housing, as the baby-boom generation forms families and turns its desires on owning conventional single family detached homes with a yard, and all the amenities such a purchase entails. To tell these young people that they may never be able to buy their own conventional single family detached home is like eliminating baseball, apple pie, and hotdogs; to destroy part of the American way of life.

It is our belief that the United States is currently experiencing the rumbling of a new era in housing. It will be an era in which many people will be living in mobile homes, townhouses, apartments, and small single family homes partially constructed in factories. Fewer and fewer families will be able to live in the large energy-inefficient conventional single family detached dwellings which are so highly valued in our society. But such a transition will not be an easy one, and may take decades before its completion.

If this is an accurate picture of things to come, exciting possibilities emerge for policymakers, researchers, teachers, interior designers, home builders, and others involved with the field of housing. A wave of innovations in the housing field is almost certain, as efforts will be required to convert unpopular housing situations into acceptable ones. Policymakers and researchers must explore what is acceptable to people and then implement programs to ensure that acceptability. Housing is rapidly becoming a critical area for serious thought.

Where will Americans live in the future? Unfortunately, there exists no neatly packaged answer to this question. What will the single family home look like in the future? Will we become a nation of renters? Will an ever-increasing number of Americans live in mobile homes, modular homes, apartments, or homes which are only on some planner's drawing board? It is our purpose in this book to offer an answer to the fundamental question: In what kinds of homes will Americans live? In our search for an answer, we begin by examining different approaches to the study of housing and then specifying our approach of focusing on housing preferences.

DIVERGENT HOUSING PERSPECTIVES

To a vast majority of Americans, housing represents more than just shelter. As the most immediate aspect of one's community living experience, it shapes people's lives. As stated by Winston Churchill following World War II: "We shape our buildings, and afterwards our buildings shape us" (quoted in Merton, 1948:204). Housing reflects status in the community, can promote or hinder family relations, serves as a major investment, and incorporates important societal values. At the same time it is the frequent object for expression of people's drive for improvement, and thus influences well-being in all dimensions of life.

Given the critical role that housing plays in people's lives, it is surprising that housing has received relatively little attention from sociologists, as well as other social scientists, in the past. Although a handful of sociologists was concerned with housing as a social problem in the years immediately following World War II (Brunsman, 1947; Chapin, 1947; Merton, 1948; Riemer, 1947; Wirth, 1947), interest waned until only recently. As a result there has been a paucity of literature addressing the social aspects of housing, which includes such topics as housing preferences, housing satisfactions, housing frustrations, housing norms, and the effects of housing on human behavior.

Wirth (1947:137) was the first sociologist to explicitly define housing as a topic appropriate for sociological study:

This discipline (sociology) is concerned with what is true of man by virtue of the fact that he leads a group life. What sociologists must discover about housing, therefore, is all those aspects which are factors in and products of man's involvement in social life. At first glance, this may seem to be initially everything, for the politics and economics of housing, as well as art, architecture and law, business, financing and administration, designing and planning, are also factors in and products of social relations.

The precise manner by which sociologists have examined housing since Wirth's initial description of the sociology of housing has been multi-faceted. Indeed, in terms of theoretical approaches, all three major sociological perspectives have been utilized to some extent in the examination of housing.

Several sociologists have approached the study of housing from the functional perspective. Early attempts include those by Chapin (1947), Dean (1953), Merton (1948), and Rossi *study housing from a functional perspective*

(1955). More recent attempts include those by Gutman (1970) and Morris and Winter (1978). The basic question addressed by these scholars is: What are the consequences of housing, and what effect does housing have on the social system as a whole? The work of Morris and Winter (1978) exemplifies this approach for examining housing. Their focus is on viewing the family as a social system that consciously evaluates its housing conditions against cultural norms. When there is a gap between actual and expected housing conditions, the family becomes dissatisfied. The result of this dissatisfaction is an attempt to reduce it by either adjustment behavior (i.e., moving to a new home or making alterations in the present home) or adaptation behavior (i.e., alteration of family norms, composition, or organization). Thus, families within a given society continuously attempt to "fit" housing to their particular needs in a rational manner; or, in other words, to achieve an equilibrium.

The conflict perspective has been preferred by those studying housing as a social problem or as a policy issue. Some of the conflicts which have attracted the attention of sociologists are those between builders and consumers, urbanites and suburbanites, minority groups and majority groups, and federal government and local government. Sociologists employing the conflict perspective perceive housing as a scarce object which people desire. Since the supply of adequate housing (as viewed by members of a society) is limited, those who gain control of it want to protect their own interests at other people's expense. Thus, the major question addressed is: Whose interests are involved in housing and who benefits or suffers from existing housing arrangements? Saltman (1975) has found that one reason discrimination exists in housing is that whites prefer racial segregation in their neighborhoods, primarily to maintain the value of their homes. In this case whites clearly benefit from housing discrimination, while blacks suffer. Anderson (1964) and Taggart (1970) have noted that many federally funded housing programs benefit the housing industry at the expense of consumers. Again, a basic conflict exists which results in differential rewards. Other examples of the utility of the conflict perspective are found in Aaron (1972), Gans (1965), Grier (1967), Lazin (1976), and Payne and Payne (1977).

A small number of sociologists have studied housing from an interactionist perspective. This perspective focuses on the everyday social interaction that takes place as people go about their daily lives. Sociologists employing the interactionist perspective in their study of housing have asked: What kinds of interactions are taking place between people, and how does the immediate environment affect these interactions? Lennard and Lennard (1977) have demonstrated that interactions between family members can become strained as a result of living in close quarters or in housing which is not well insulated in terms of noise. Kushell (1977) has suggested that residents of public housing develop a frustrated and negative view of themselves as a consequence of living in housing that represents failure in the eyes of society, and this leads to particular kinds of interaction with others. Other instances of the usefulness of the interactionist perspective in studying housing are found in Cooper (1972; 1975) and Goffman (1959).

Recently a new sociological specialty labeled environmental sociology has developed which provides useful insights regarding the social aspects of housing. Dunlap and Catton (1979:244) state that environmental sociology "involves recognition of the fact that physical environments can influence (and in turn be influenced by) human societies and behavior." These physical environments range from pristine to modified to built environments. Housing is one type of the built environment, and can be studied by examining its interactions with the societal variables of population, technology, cultural system, social system, and personality system. There has already been a considerable amount of research directed at examining the effects that housing has on society (see, e.g., Heimstra and McFarling, 1978; Michelson, 1977; Sommer, 1974a) and the effects that society has on housing (see, e.g., Newmark and Thompson, 1977; Wilson, 1967). All three of the above theoretical frameworks can be utilized in an environmental sociology approach to housing.

In addition to categorizing the sociology of housing literature according to the implicit and explicit theoretical perspectives held by authors, it is possible to distinguish between topical issues of concern. In doing so, it is important to recognize that not all work in the sociology of housing area has been conducted by sociologists. Architects, community planners, psychologists, political scientists, lawyers, and home economists have all made valuable contributions to an understanding of the social aspects of housing.

Tremblay, et al. (1978) have divided the sociology of housing literature into four categories. The first category concerns the social and psychological effects of housing environments. Publications within this category generally revolve around answering the questions of why housing is important as a variable in sociological analysis (Gutman, 1970; Merton, 1948; Wirth, 1947), and how housing affects human behavior (Booth, 1976; Loo, 1978; Mitchell, 1974; Smith, et al., 1969; Sommer, 1974b). Much of the literature in this category involves measuring the effects that density or crowding have on behavior.

Assessing the quality of housing is the focal point of another set of literature. It deals with measuring both the objective quality (Duhl, 1963; Lakshmanan, et al., 1976; Obudho, 1976; Shinn, 1971; Sumka, 1977) and subjective quality (Becker, 1974; Hartman, 1963; Hinshaw and Allott, 1972; McKown, 1975; Michelson, 1967; Morris and Winter, 1978; Williams, 1971) of housing. In terms of assessing the subjective quality of housing, variables such as preferences, satisfactions, frustrations, and expectations have been considered.

Third, a great deal of research has been reported which examines housing problems which appear to be unique to certain segments of the population. Those groups of people found to have special housing needs and problems on the basis of their measured objective and/or subjective housing quality include the elderly (Gelwicks and Newcomer, 1974; Huttman, 1977), poor (Grimes, 1976), handicapped (Olsen and Meredith, 1973); minorities (Hawkins, 1976), rural residents (Bird and Kampe, 1977; Select Committee on Nutrition and Human Needs, 1971), and inner-city residents (Manvel, 1968).

Finally, housing policy has been reviewed and critically evaluated by researchers publishing in the sociology of housing area. Some topics of interest in this regard are the formulation and implementation of housing policy (Carlton and Ferreira, 1977; Hartman, 1975; Meehan, 1975), feasibility of policy (Greendale and Knock, 1976; Prescott, 1975; Solomon, 1974), and impact of policy (Aaron, 1972; Downs, 1974; Lord, 1977; Welfeld, 1977; Yearns, 1978).

A FOCUS ON HOUSING PREFERENCES

The focus of this book is one specific aspect of the sociology of housing--namely, housing preferences. Housing preferences can be utilized as measures of subjective housing quality; therefore, they fall within the topical area of housing quality assessment. We can conceive of housing preferences as reflecting the level of desirability directed at various housing situations. Thus, it is possible to state that a particular housing situation is preferred or is not preferred by an individual or a group. Housing situations refer to a variety of combinations of housing structure types and housing tenure statuses. Basic housing structure types are conventional single family detached homes, mobile homes, duplexes, townhouses, and apartments. The two types of housing tenure status are ownership and tenancy. Housing situations, therefore, include such possibilities as owning a conventional single family detached home, renting an apartment, and owning a mobile home on rented space. We can conclude that housing preferences connote the kind of home in which people want to live.

At this juncture it is necessary to distinguish the concept of housing preferences from three similar concepts--housing expectations, aspirations, and norms. As defined by Morris and Winter (1978:40), expectations are a: "Realistic assessment of future conditions or behavior . . . what is felt to be plausible in the future." Aspirations are: "Desires or norms oriented toward the future." Norms are: "A set of rules or ideals for behavior and conditions . . . ." Thus, there exist norms in our society which prescribe the kinds of housing situations in which people should live. Unfortunately, some people cannot satisfy the dominant housing norms due to certain constraints (e.g., inadequate income), and aspire towards satisfying those norms. Expectations can be thought of as aspirations which are modified based on current constraints; reasonable hopes of at least partially satisfying the dominant housing norms.

In this book a strict distinction between housing preferences, aspirations, and expectations is not enforced, primarily because the literature rarely differentiates between the three concepts. In fact, it is often difficult to determine whether a particular study is examining housing preferences, aspirations, or expectations. More importantly, the three concepts are generally addressing the same question: In what kind of home do people wish to live? Conversely, housing preferences are sharply differentiated from housing norms. Housing norms determine what people want to obtain in their housing environments. If society has a norm for home ownership, then members of that society will attempt to conform to the norm by buying a home. Housing preferences are the specific forms by which the housing norms are expressed. Thus, a preference for owning a conventional single family detached house may be an expression of the norms for home ownership and conventional single family detached dwelling.

The overriding theoretical perspective to be employed here is functionalism. By using this approach, housing preferences are viewed as emerging out of people's interaction with others in the social structure. One result of being a member of a society is that there are pressures to conform to the norms of that society. And, every society has norms, along with associated sanctions, which directly influence people's housing behavior. Members of a society constantly judge their current housing situation with the housing norms. If the two are in equilibrium, then no action will be undertaken to change one's current housing situation on the basis of the housing norms. If housing conditions do not conform to the norms, behavior will be exerted to attain a housing situation which does comply with the norms. All societal members seek social rewards, such as respect and prestige, and avoid social punishments, such as ridicule. The rewards derive from norm conformance, while punishments derive from deviance from the norms. Thus, housing behavior seeks to comply with the dominant housing norms. The housing situation which best meets the housing norms within a given society should therefore be the preferred housing situation.

An assumption of functionalism is that there is a high degree of value consensus within a society. This assumption implies that the dominant housing norms apply equally to all societal members. However, humans obviously differ on a number of personal and social characteristics, and these differences exist within any society. An argument can be developed suggesting that the housing norms apply differentially depending upon an individual's or a group's place in society. Characteristics which might result in the holding of different norms are marital status, age, income, education, and sex. Therefore, personal characteristics must be considered along with housing norms when analyzing housing preferences. As suggested by Hinshaw and Allott (1972:102): "Preferential responses must . . . be evaluated in light of the particular socioeconomic setting of the respondents."

Based on the above discussion, it appears that two approaches can be utilized in attempting to explain why people prefer to live in one housing situation as opposed to another. One approach is to focus on the personal characteristics of people as factors influencing housing preferences. A second approach is to focus on the attributes of particular housing situations as the basis for the differential level of preference directed at those housing situations. In other words, what is the role of housing norms in determining housing preferences? In this book the two approaches are combined in an effort to provide a more complete understanding of people's stated housing preferences and the underlying reasons for the existence of those preferences.

Our analysis of housing preferences derives from an extensive review of the relevant literature and the results of a mail survey conducted in Washington state. The survey assessed the extent to which 2,801 households would prefer to live in seven commonly available housing situations: own a single family home, rent a single family home, own a mobile home and lot, own a mobile home on rented space, own a townhouse, rent a duplex, and rent an apartment. Data were also collected on a variety of personal characteristics which provide indicators of housing location, current housing situation, household composition, and social class.

2

The Why and How of Studying Housing Preferences

It is widely assumed that for a majority of Americans ownership of a single family dwelling constitutes an ideal (Cooper, 1972). Further, such an ideal is assumed to transcend the housing preferences of various segments of the population (Morris and Winter, 1976). While there has been some speculation that the preference for single family home ownership may be on the decline (see, e.g., Packard, 1972), studies indicate that despite the high costs and high resource use involved, Americans still desire to own a detached single family home surrounded by a plot of land (Breckenfeld, 1976; Winter and Morris, 1977). The study most often cited in support of this preference is a national survey of metropolitan residents conducted more than 15 years ago (Michelson, 1967). The results of this study revealed virtually no interest in moving from single family dwellings to multiple family dwellings. More recent research has produced similar results, indicating "that the desire for single family home ownership is ubiquitous and not in the process of radically changing" (Hinshaw and Allott, 1972: 107).

LIMITATIONS OF PAST RESEARCH

A careful review of the literature reveals that we actually have little evidence regarding American housing preferences. While it is true that numerous studies have sought an answer to this question (see Tremblay, et al., 1978:Section II), they suffer from certain shortcomings. Specifically, past studies have exhibited two important deficiencies: sampling problems and an expression of preferences based upon a range of choices substantially more limited than the housing situations presently available. As a result, we have only a sketchy notion of people's housing preferences.

In our review of the housing preference literature we could locate no study that surveyed a representative sample of the entire United States or even one state. The study which came closest to such generalizability is Michelson's (1967) classic study which consisted of a national sample of metropolitan area residents only, and which therefore ignored all nonmetropolitan residents. Other studies are even more limited, ranging from general public samples in single counties (Belcher, 1970) or cities (Morris and Winter, 1976), to highly specialized samples of low-income people (McCray and Day, 1977; Williams, 1971) or college students (Hinshaw and Allott, 1972; Montgomery and Kivlin, 1962). Other studies have reported the housing preferences of undergraduate architecture students (Canter and Thorne, 1972), student couples in north central Missouri (McKown, 1975), mothers living in college married-student housing (Thornburg, 1975), Minneapolis families (Caplow, 1948), home owners in Detroit (Rosow, 1948), home shoppers in southern California (Gerardi, 1976), and Italian- and Irish-Americans (Michelson, 1966). Although there is nothing intrinsically wrong with using such samples, they obviously cannot provide a clear impression of the housing preferences of the general American public.

The utility of previous studies has also been jeopardized by small samples. The largest sample located in our review of the housing preference literature was 1,947 (Montgomery and Kivlin, 1962), while the smallest was 26 (McKown, 1975). A majority of the studies have employed samples of less than 100 people. One result of such small samples is that the results reported may be biased. We would have more confidence in the findings of previous studies if the samples were larger. Another result of such small samples is that detailed analyses to identify the preferences of various segments of the population (e.g., people under 30 or single person households) have not been conducted. Such analyses are of considerable importance inasmuch as the preferences of a relatively small, but identifiable, portion of the population may provide adequate market incentives for production of housing neither preferred nor suited for the vast majority of Americans.

Furthermore, a variety of question formats have been employed to assess housing preferences. For example, Morris and Winter (1976) asked questions concerning the best kind of housing for the respondent's own family at the present time; Michelson (1967) asked questions on what kind of home respondents wanted; Williams (1971) showed respondents color slides and asked them whether the home displayed in each slide was preferred or acceptable; Hinshaw and Allott (1972) asked what kind of home respondents would prefer in ten years; and Ladd (1972) asked respondents to verbally describe their ideal home.

Others (e.g., McCray and Day, 1977; McKown, 1975; Zey-Ferrell, et al., 1977) have taken a much narrower perspective on housing preferences, and have measured very specific kinds of preferences. Still other researchers never report the manner in which they measured housing preferences. Thus, the failure to replicate the same question in numerous surveys renders it difficult to compensate for the limitations of the sample frame employed in a given study.

Equally frustrating is the limited range of housing alternatives that have been examined in the housing preference literature. At a minimum people in search of housing are confronted by decisions concerning varying tenure status options (own versus rent) as well as a large number of basic housing structure types (e.g., apartment buildings, duplex units, mobile homes, townhouses, and single family homes). Yet, no one study has systematically assessed the level of preference directed at each of the extant viable housing options. For example, Belcher (1970), Ladd (1972), Michelson (1967; 1968), Thornburg (1975), and Williams (1971) present data on a limited number of structure type preferences, without examining tenure status preferences simultaneously. Other studies report tenure status preferences while neglecting the structure type variable (Caplow, 1948; Montgomery and McCabe, 1973; Rosow, 1948). Even those few studies which do analyze both structure type and tenure status preferences are restricted in their value because they report data on single family home ownership preferences, thereby excluding consideration of alternative housing situations (Morris and Winter, 1976). Indeed, only two studies adequately consider a variety of housing structure types other than the conventional single family detached dwelling (Hinshaw and Allott, 1972; Williams, 1971). And, one of these (Williams, 1971) neglects consideration of the conventional single family detached home in his study.

Thus, one reason for conducting further research into the area of housing preferences is to overcome the problems afflicting previous research (summarized in Table 1). The purpose of this book is to present data from a survey assessing housing preferences in which an effort has been exerted to overcome each of these problems. Specifically, we will report data collected via a statewide mail survey of 2,801 Washington residents in which respondents were asked to choose from among seven housing situations (which take into account both structure type and tenure status) selected to represent the most common options available.

Table 1. Summary of the Relevant Housing Preference Literature

Study	Sample Frame[a]	Sample Size[b]	Housing Alternatives[c]
Hinshaw and Allott (1972)	College students	204	Tenure/structure (3)
Montgomery and McCabe (1973)	Low income--local	501	Tenure
Morris and Winter (1976)	City residents	372	Tenure/structure (1)
Michelson (1966)	Italian- or Irish-Americans	75	Structure (1)
Michelson (1967)	National-metropolitan residents	748	Structure (2)
McCray and Day (1977)	Low income--local	79	Structure (1)
Williams (1971)	Low income--city	217	Structure (4)
Montgomery and Kivlin (1962)	College students	1947	Structure (1)
Caplow (1948)	City residents	574	Tenure
Rosow (1948)	City homeowners	33	Tenure
Ladd (1972)	Junior high students	60	Structure (1)
Rushing (1970)	State--farmers and farm laborers	1211	Tenure
McKown (1975)	Couples--local	26	Structure (1)
Canter and Thorne (1972)	College students	92	Structure (3)
Belcher (1970)	County residents	540	Structure (1)
Thornburg (1975)	College students	67	Structure (2)
Gerardi (1976)	Home shoppers	700	Structure (1)

[a]The most descriptive term is used to label the sample frame.

[b]Sample size listed is the number of respondents employed in the study's analysis.

[c]Housing alternatives listed are those actually reported in the study. Number in parentheses represents the different structure types examined.

WHY STUDY HOUSING PREFERENCES?

In addition to the need for further research on housing preferences which overcomes the deficiencies inherent in previous research, there are five reasons why housing preferences should be subjected to detailed study. Specifically, it is crucial to examine housing preferences because of rapidly increasing housing costs, changes in the availability of some housing resources, importance of housing in the quality of life experienced by Americans, potential policy impact, and influence on actual housing behavior.

Housing Costs

For many Americans hopes of owning a conventional single family detached home may be a vanishing dream, as they find themselves being priced out of their preferred housing market. Indeed, the price of housing has escalated to the point where even a "modest" home cannot be purchased by the average-income American family unless it sacrifices other family needs. Some families may sacrifice food, clothing, and educational goals to own a home. Breckenfeld (1976:84-85) reports that in 1975 only about four out of ten American families could afford the payments on the median-priced house, based on the rule of thumb that a family can afford a home 2.5 times its gross yearly income. In a more pessimistic statement, Cleere (1979:3) suggests that three-quarters of the American families cannot afford a median-priced home.

There are two factors behind the growing difficulty that many American families experience when attempting to purchase a conventional single family detached home. The first factor is the rising price of single family houses. In 1971, the median-price of new homes sold was $25,200, while in 1981 it increased to $68,800 (National Association of Home Builders, 1982:6). The picture is much the same regarding existing homes, as median-prices increased from $24,800 in 1971 to $66,400 in 1981 (National Association of Home Builders, 1982:6). During this period, median-prices rose 173 percent for new homes and 170 percent for existing homes. The housing price situation does vary across communities. Of 32 major metropolitan areas surveyed by the Federal Home Loan Bank Board in 1981, the median-price of all homes sold ranged from a high of $127,300 in San Francisco to a low of $60,300 in St. Louis (National Association of Home Builders, 1982:7).

The second factor is median-family income. If people's income kept pace with the escalation of housing prices then there would not be as much of a housing problem. However, income has failed to keep pace with housing prices. For example, the median-price of new single family homes increased 105 percent between 1972 and 1978, while median-family income increased 57 percent (U.S. News and World Report, 1979:54). A growing number of Americans cannot afford a new conventional single family detached home, and the problem continues to grow each year. To amplify this point, we can compare median-family income and median-sales prices of new single family homes. Using the rule of thumb that a family can afford a home 2.5 times its yearly income, the average family (median-income of about $23,000 in 1982) could not afford the median-priced home.

To make matters worse, mortgage interest rates are reaching record highs. In one decade they increased from about 6 percent to an average of 10.5 percent (Egan, 1977:9). Recently, mortgage interest rates have gone well over the 10.5 percent figure in most states, and even reached 20 percent in the winter of 1980. Every one-percent increase in the mortgage interest rate has significant ramifications, as it takes approximately 2.9 million families out of the housing market (Cleere, 1979:3). As an example of the effects of an increase in interest rates, the New Republic (1975:6) calculates that a 2 percent difference in a mortgage for a $40,000 home (25 percent down, with 25 year maturity) means $40 more each month, or $480 a year. Similarly, the National Association of Home Builders calculates a $180 difference in total monthly expenses between a 30 year term, $60,000 fixed-rate mortgage at 10 percent interest ($742 a month) and one at 14 percent interest ($926 a month) (National Association of Home Builders, 1982:9). Obviously, the increase in mortgage interest rates is contributing to the difficulties of purchasing a conventional single family detached home.

As a result of the rising costs associated with purchasing a conventional single family detached home, new home purchases appear to be reserved for those families which are previous home owners, have both spouses employed, or can obtain money for a down payment from relatives. Jacobs, an economist with the United States League of Savings Associations, states that 45 percent of the home buyers in 1977 were two-income families. According to a June 4, 1980 report by the United States League of Savings Associations, that figure increased to 54 percent in 1979. Further, the report states that only 18 percent of all home buyers were purchasing their first home (U.S. News and World Report, 1980:12). Thus, most of those buying homes already are home owners. Another concern is that in order to raise a down payment which is typically 20 percent of the home's value, many families are borrowing heavily from relatives. The family or single adult who lacks these financial sources which are needed for the purchase of a conventional single family detached home may well be out of their preferred housing market.

This situation is of great concern because an increase in the population of potential home buyers is creating a substantial demand for conventional single family detached homes. Those born during the post World War II baby boom are now reaching the home-buying age. As stated in U.S. News and World Report (1979:54): "Behind the price worries that tomorrow's home buyers will face is the sheer number of people looking for shelter. In the 1980s, an estimated 42 million Americans will reach the prime home-buying age of 30, compared with only 32 million in the '70s." To illustrate the fact that the age of 30 is significant in terms of home ownership, Breckenfeld (1976:87-88) reports that 20 percent of those between 20 and 24 years of age own their home, compared to 60 percent of those between 30 and 34. Thus, changes in the demographic structure of the United States will create a substantial demand for single family home ownership, particularly during the next decade. Winter and Morris (1977:9) suggest that this will be similar to the demand placed on apartments a few years ago. Now the apartment dwellers are reaching an age where owning a conventional single family detached house is likely desired.

If this growing number of Americans is unable to secure their preferred housing environment, questions arise concerning a future society comprised of couples rearing their children in small multiple family dwellings or mobile homes. And, these housing options may well have some serious drawbacks for some people. For example, family conflict may be higher in small apartments than in large conventional single family detached homes, and the poor insulation in most mobile homes may create difficulties in sleeping (Lennard and Lennard, 1977). To emphasize the point that multiple family homes have serious drawbacks, Thornburg (1975:192) suggests that: "Close proximity to neighbors and lack of private space surrounding the living unit may force the restraining of a child's freedom to move beyond the interior of the living unit. Such constraints could foster over-dependency in the child and delay the development of autonomous behavior during the pre-school years." Thus, if families cannot afford a conventional single family detached home which they can own, there may be serious consequences regarding family functioning. Further, there may be a psychological problem regarding families living in housing environments which they find frustrating with no prospects for improvement.

Availability of Housing Resources

Due to the rising costs of owning a conventional single family detached house, living in alternative types of housing becomes a very real possibility confronting many Americans. Given the substantial demands placed on energy, community services, and natural resources by conventional single family detached homes, the likelihood of living in multiple family dwellings or mobile homes increases. Thus, shortages of many resources on which the conventional single family detached home is dependent constitutes the second reason for carefully studying housing preferences.

Since the 1973-1974 oil embargo, the United States has recognized that petroleum energy is not as plentiful or inexpensive as it once was. In efforts to curb energy consumption, the energy efficiency of conventional single family detached homes has been carefully examined. Newman and Day (1975:Table 1-7) state that about 20 percent of this nation's energy is consumed by the residential sector. This is a significant amount of energy, and the proportion of energy used in homes has increased approximately 5 percent since 1950 compared to other energy consuming sectors, such as agriculture, industry, and military (Schurr, 1971:11). One way to reduce heavy home energy consumption is to discourage single family home ownership, and encourage life in multiple family dwellings. It is a fact that conventional single family detached homes are typically inefficient in terms of energy use because "each home must provide for its own individual heating and cooling systems, electrical appliances, and be enclosed by four walls and a roof which let out warm air in the winter and cool air in the summer" (Dillman, et al., 1977:3).

The rising costs of energy for heating and cooling homes is an indication of the increasing scarcity of this needed resource. Morrison, et al. (1977:6) found that between 1974 and 1976 fuel oil increased in price by 126 percent and natural gas increased in cost by 81 percent in the state of Michigan. The recent process of deregulating the price of natural gas has dramatically increased the cost of heating homes for many American families. A doubling of natural gas bills from one winter to the next has been common. Given such price increases many home owners will be hard pressed to heat and cool their homes in the fashion in which they have become accustomed. Thus, rising energy costs may provide American families with an incentive to live in multiple family dwellings or mobile homes.

The conventional single family detached home places an exceedingly heavy demand on community services, which are becoming more limited due to inflationary pressures. Low density single family developments require communities to provide streets, utilities, protective services, and a high quality of life in general for their residents (Clapperton and Carreiro, 1972; Hoben, 1975). Further, each house must be provided road access, sewage hookups, water and storm drainage facilities, as well as pipes and lines for utilities. Services of the same quality can be provided to multiple family dwellings at a much more efficient cost. In addition, some communities are purposely limiting their population growth and expansion in order to avoid costly additions of various services (e.g., schools, sewer, water, and fire protection). Thus, it may be more difficult for new single family homes to receive community services once taken for granted (Time, 1973).

Land is one resource which is becoming increasingly scarce. Indeed, the most significant reason for rising home costs is rising land prices: in 1975 land comprised 26 percent of the cost for single family homes (Breckenfeld, 1976:89). Besides the fact that good land is becoming more scarce, local building restrictions have further reduced the number and size of available plots (New Republic, 1975:6). Thus, the scarcity of land on which to build encourages the growth of the multiple family dwelling industry at the expense of the conventional single family detached home industry. And considering the expanding American population, it seems more efficient and ecologically desirable to cluster housing in a small portion of land, rather than spreading them out on their own lots.

Several building materials have become more difficult to obtain in recent years, and this is reflected in their increased cost. Significant price increases have occurred for five of the major housing components: Douglas fir, plywood, millwork, paint, and asphalt roofing (Morris and Winter, 1978:Table 13). The rapid increase in wood prices is partially a result of their growing scarcity, as forests are unable to produce wood as fast as the rising demand for lumber. The increase in the cost of asphalt roofing and paint is a direct result of the scarcity of petroleum. As stated by the President of the National Association of Home Builders, lumber prices went up 30 percent, glass increased 8 percent, and aluminum jumped 10 percent during 1982, a reflection of resource availability. Multiple family dwellings and mobile homes require fewer building materials to house more people than do conventional single family detached homes. Thus, shortages in some building materials increases the probability of Americans living in alternative housing structure types.

The implications of scarcity are clear: the conventional single family detached home is typically inefficient and should be replaced by more efficient housing, such as mobile homes and multiple family dwellings. This suggests that we may be entering a new era of housing selection, one in which the crucial question is not how to meet people's first preferences, but how to provide for a less preferred choice.

Quality of Life

Another reason for examining housing preferences derives from research conducted on the quality of life experienced by Americans. In recent years social scientists have pondered the question of what provides for quality of life, and in doing so have focused their concern on subjective factors (see, e.g., Andrews and Withey, 1976). A subjective approach to quality of life attempts to reveal the factors contributing to happiness, satisfaction, and contentment. One of the major factors found to be related to perceived life quality is housing.

Andrews and Withey (1976:Chapter 5) found a strong relationship between housing satisfaction and total life satisfaction. From a rather lengthy list of possible predictors of life quality, feelings about home and apartment ranked fifth as a predictor of a sense of well-being and life satisfaction, ranking behind only personal concerns such as self-efficacy and family life. Campbell et al. (1976:265), also found that housing is related to expressed satisfaction with life as a whole. In fact, they found that: "The most powerful determinant of the wish to move . . . is the satisfaction with one's current dwelling unit (Campbell, et al., 1976:261). Rossi (1955) reports data consistent with those of Campbell and his associates, indicating that housing is the most frequently given reason for moving. These findings suggest that efforts to improve quality of life by moving are strongly related to housing.

The fact that housing is an important component of quality of life should not be surprising inasmuch as the home is the most immediate aspect of our living experiences and as such shapes our lives. Indeed, Beyer (1965:308) stated that housing is "the one area that probably affects us most immediately and directly." Specifically, people spend much of their day in the confines of their homes; the home separates people from others; the home provides a place of retreat for replenishment made necessary by the high stimulation environment experienced in our technical society; the home represents socio-economic status in the eyes of the community; and housing costs demand a large piece of the family budget pie (Dillman and Tremblay, 1977:123; Michelson, 1976:356; Montgomery, 1970:270-271).

The relationship between housing and quality of life implies that a worsening of housing conditions may adversely affect perceived life quality. Thus, if people's housing preferences cannot be attained, satisfaction with their housing as well as their total life quality may decline. Given that satisfaction is strongly related to owning a conventional single family detached house (Morris and Winter, 1978:158), and that it is this housing situation which is most endangered by rising housing costs and scarcity of critical housing resources, there is reason to believe that perceived life quality may decline in the future. Thus, it is crucial to determine precisely the housing preferences of Americans.

Public Policy

A fourth reason for studying housing preferences is that a knowledge of such preferences is important for policy purposes. To the extent that the opportunity to live in the housing environment of our choice is threatened, and for the first time in our lives it is now being severely threatened, pressure will be exerted to alleviate the problem. We expect a government response to this pressure on the basis of its often-stated goal of providing "A decent home and suitable living environment for every American family." Also, as suggested by Michelson (1968:38): "in a democratic and open society like ours, popular preferences are ignored only at great peril." Such a government response might be of varying forms: loans to buy single family homes, experimental mortgage programs, control on the ceiling of mortgage interest rates, incentives to move into multiple family dwellings or mobile homes, elimination of some federal building regulations, and pressure on the private housing industry to trim construction costs (Hartman, 1975; Solomon, 1974). Of course, many new policy forms dealing with the housing problem will emerge in the future.

Unfortunately, government will be asked to accomplish several tasks simultaneously, some of which may not be compatible with one another. For example, government will be asked to protect the substantial investments present home owners have in their homes (i.e., allow them to realize a profit if they sell) while at the same time keeping the cost of housing within the reach of most families. Regardless of the policies developed and implemented by government, many will not be taken lightly. Thus, when government granted low down payment and low-interest loans to lower-class blacks in New York, many middle-class whites who could not afford homes were upset (Williams, 1978). When apartment complexes were being built at a rapid pace during the early 1970s, supported to some degree by government, it was not realized that this was to be only temporary housing for the baby-boom generation (Winter and Morris, 1977:8-9). The policies to be formulated, then, would undoubtedly benefit from research depicting the kinds of homes in which people prefer to live.

However, a single policy response often ends up in the long run being worse than no response at all (Hartman, 1975:159-163). If we find that the majority of American families prefer to own conventional single family detached homes, a policy to make this preference universally attainable will not be welcomed by everybody. In short, a general housing policy designed to meet the needs of all Americans appears to be impractical. A better direction for government is the development of a series of housing policies based on the particular segments of the population at which they would be directed. Families vary in size, education, income, place of residence, and age among other characteristics. Thus, a home may be required to fulfill quite different functions according to the composition of the household. For example, a large family has much more flexibility in terms of housing choice. Different households also have varying needs in terms of accessibility to community services, transportation, and open space (Morris and Winter, 1975; Rossi, 1955). Housing policies should take these differing needs into account. Therefore, specific (or more limited) housing policies designed to entail the differing needs based on household composition appear to be a more practical way to effect meaningful social change in the realm of housing. Only by understanding people's housing preferences can such policies be successfully formulated and implemented.

Housing Behavior

We expect that the manner in which people select their home is influenced by their preferences. If a family states a preference for owning a conventional single family detached home, then it will probably engage in behavior which is directed at satisfying that preference. Although the behavior may not be sufficient to attain the preferred housing situation (due to factors such as inadequate income or difficulties in obtaining a mortgage in a tight-money market), there is an attempt to do so based on held housing preferences. The important point is that one's preference predisposes one to behave in a particular manner.

There has been a substantial amount of research indicating that the attitude- (a preference is a type of attitude) behavior relationship is an ambiguous one (see, e.g., Schuman and Johnson, 1976). However, there have been studies revealing a strong relationship between attitudes and behavior (e.g., Kelly and Mirer, 1974). Unfortunately, there has been only one study, to our knowledge, that has examined the relationship between housing preferences and housing behavior (Michelson, 1977). In that study it was found that over a period of time people attempted to obtain housing satisfying their preferences. As stated by Michelson (1977:364), "what people say they want and prefer is very highly related to what they try to and succeed in getting for themselves at a later point in time . . . ." Related research dealing with housing imagery (i.e., images people have of their desired home) suggests that housing imagery significantly influences actual housing behavior (Boulding, 1956:Chapter 4; Montgomery and McCabe, 1973:8). Since preferences reflect people's images of desirable housing for themselves and their families, they should also reflect predispositions to behave in a particular manner when selecting a home.

METHODS FOR THIS STUDY

Survey research has been the primary method for studying housing preferences. This is not surprising given that most researchers want to extrapolate their findings from a sample to a population. Experimental and participant observation study designs are not as appropriate for this purpose. Further, the most popular type of survey used in the past has been the face-to-face interview. Due to the cost and expertise in interviewing skills demanded by face-to-face surveys, sample frames and the size of samples have been quite limited in previous research. In order to discover the housing preferences of a general population, the mail survey method may prove more effective.

The Survey

The mail survey seems particularly appealing for studying housing preferences because of recent improvements of the method. Several techniques developed by Dillman (1978) have produced response rates competitive with those obtained in face-to-face interviews (70 to 75 percent), but at much lower cost. Other problems that have previously curtailed extensive use of mail surveys (e.g., difficulty of asking complex questions and length of questionnaire) have been proven to be not nearly as severe as once thought.

An approach for conducting mail surveys which can successfully attain high quality and quantity of data has been termed the "Total Design Method" by Dillman (1978). The underlying principle behind the Total Design Method is that each aspect of the survey process must be designed in such a way that the respondent will receive a favorable impression of both the research and the researcher. By manipulating each aspect of the survey, the end result should be a survey which has the most favorable overall effect on the respondent.

With the utilization of the Total Design Method, a well packaged and administered survey results. The questionnaire consists of a well-designed cover letter, an attractive front cover (e.g., eye-catching drawing), a useful back cover to end the questionnaire (e.g., thanking respondents for participating in the survey and providing an opportunity for them to request a copy of the results), questionnaire pages of high readability accomplished through a multilithing process, and carefully constructed and ordered questions, all of which are put into a booklet format. With reminders and replacement questionnaires strategically placed according to the administrative plan (e.g., postcard reminder one week after original mailout, replacement questionnaire two weeks later, and a second replacement questionnaire three weeks later), overall excellent results can be achieved.

The data reported in this book were collected via the Total Design Method for mail surveys. In the summer of 1977, questionnaires were mailed to a representative sample of 4,500 Washington households. These households were systematically drawn from all the telephone directories in the state. Since 93 percent of the households in Washington State have access to telephones (U.S. Bureau of the Census, 1976:534), the use of telephone directories as the sampling frame was deemed appropriate. All counties and communities in the state were represented in the sample in proportion to the number of residents living in each. Of the 4,500 households mailed a questionnaire, 417 were disqualified (i.e., the intended respondent was either deceased, disabled such that he or she could not fill out the questionnaire, had moved out of state, or had moved without leaving a forwarding address). Of the remaining 4,083 households, complete questionnaires were obtained from 2,801 households. This figure constitutes a 68.6 percent response rate.

The questionnaire was 12 pages in length. However, the questionnaire was printed in a booklet format and contained 10 pages of primarily closed-ended questions. A two-page insert to collect information from a second adult member of the household was also included with the questionnaire. The use of an insert was probably responsible for the slightly lower response rate than is normally obtained using the Total Design Method. This possible explanation is supported by Carpenter (1977:252), who found a significant reduction in response rate when two members, as opposed to one member, of a household were asked to complete a mail questionnaire.

There are certain biases resulting from the methods employed in this study to draw the sample and collect the data. Those who are older, less educated, renters, and/or economically deprived are generally underrepresented by mail surveys (Goudy, 1978). However, when the characteristics of the sample are compared to those of the state population few major differences emerge. As displayed in Table 2, only in the case of education is there a difference exceeding 10 percent, and this may be pronounced because of the time discrepancy in which education data were collected (1970 for state and 1977 for sample). As expected, respondents are somewhat older, and more apt to be married, home owners, and employed than the general state population. In short, respondents appear to represent a slightly more stable population than those not included in the study. Other differences are slight, especially with regard to current dwelling type and county residence. We conclude that although there are some differences in personal characteristics between respondents and those not in the study, they are relatively small. Therefore, the questionnaire responses obtained in the survey are reasonably representative of the state as a whole.

The questionnaire employed in this study covered a variety of housing concerns (see Appendix A). Respondents were first asked to describe the home in which they currently live, including its present condition, size, number and types of rooms, its value, and the cost to own or rent and maintain it. There were also several questions addressing housing satisfaction. Questions on this topic included willingness to move, the extent to which particular features of their homes were considered to be a reason for complaint, and overall satisfaction with their homes. Next, housing preferences were measured. Respondents were asked what kind of home they wanted and whether they would accept certain home energy conservation measures. The questionnaire concluded with questions on the personal characteristics of respondents and their families.

Measurement of Variables

Housing preferences constitute the dependent variables in this analysis. Housing preferences were measured by two questions. The first question asked: "Just suppose that for some reason you had to move out of your present home and you were given a chance to live in each of the places listed below during the next five years. To what extent would you consider each choice?" Response categories were "definitely no,"

Table 2.   Comparison of Characteristics of Respondents and State Population

Personal Characteristics	Sample (%)	State (%)	Percent Difference
Live in metropolitan county	72.1	71.7[a]	0.4
Age 65 or above	18.7	10.5[a]	8.2
College education	29.8	13.8[b]	16.0
Unemployed	4.4	9.5[c]	5.1
Male	55.4	49.6[c]	5.8
Married	73.2	64.1[b]	9.1
Homeowner	75.0	66.8[b]	8.2
Over 2 people in household	46.8	49.8[c]	3.0
Live in single family house	77.2	75.8[b]	1.4
Live in mobile home	6.1	3.2[b]	2.9
Live in multi-unit dwelling	15.1	21.0[b]	5.9

NOTE: Comparisons should be considered with some caution as "characteristic" categories are not always the same for the sample and the state.

[a]1976 data from Office of Program Planning and Fiscal Management, Population Studies Division, State of Washington Population Trends, 1976 (Olympia, WA: OPPFM, 1976).

[b]1970 data from U.S. Census Bureau, 1970 Census of Population: General Social and Economic Characteristics (Washington, D.C.: U.S. Government Printing Office, 1972), and U.S. Census Bureau, Housing Characteristics for States, Cities, and Counties (Washington, D.C.: U.S. Government Printing Office, 1972).

[c]1975 data from Bureau of Vital Statistics, Vital Statistics, 1975 (Olympia, WA: Washington State Department of Social and Health Services, 1976), and Office of Program Planning and Fiscal Management, Pocket Data Book, 1976 (Olympia, WA: OPPFM, 1976).

"probably no," "unsure," "probably yes," and "definitely yes."
Housing choices were as follows: "Buy a mobile home located in
a rented space in a mobile home park," "Buy a mobile home
located on a lot that you also buy," "Buy a single family
house," "Buy a townhouse (shares side wall with houses next
door)," "Rent a single family house," "Rent an apartment in a
building containing five or more other apartments," and "Rent a
unit in a duplex."

Immediately following this question, respondents were
asked: "Which of the above would you most prefer to live in?"
Respondents were instructed to put the numbers assigned to
their housing choices in two boxes, one box for "most prefer"
and a second box for "second most prefer." The responses obtained from the first question on housing preferences will be
treated as interval level data in forthcoming analyses, while the
responses obtained from the second question can be considered
as only ordinal level data and will be treated as such.

Earlier in the questionnaire drawings were employed to
give respondents a framework from which they could operation-
ally define each housing type. Thus, responses to the housing
preference questions should be quite reliable. Also, in the
housing preference choices presented to respondents, both tenure status and structure type were incorporated in various
combinations. Therefore, people's responses reflect preferences
for housing environments that differ in tenure status and/or
structure type. Choices presented to respondents are those
that best represent the actual housing situations available to
Washington residents.

The independent variables to be used in this study can be
categorized into four groups: location of present home (county
size and city size); current housing situation (structure type
and tenure status); household composition (household size, respondent's age, respondent's sex, and respondent's marital status); and social class (family income, respondent's education,
and occupation). County size was measured by asking: "In
what Washington county is your home located?" City size was
measured by asking: "What town or city do you depend on
most for goods and services?" For these questions respondents
wrote down the name of their county and city of residence,
which were then categorized according to their size.

Housing structure type was ascertained as follows: "We
would like to begin by asking you to describe the home in
which you now live. Which one of the following pictures comes
closest to describing your present home?" The pictures which
could be selected were for "apartment building," "townhouse
(shared sidewalls)," "duplex," "mobile home (single or double

wide)," "mobile home with attached structure," "apartment in a house," and "a single family house." In a question involving costs, respondents were asked to either answer items regarding renting or owning costs. Tenure status was determined by whether the respondent chose the rent or own items.

Respondents were asked to list all those currently living in their household, including themselves. Household size was determined by the number of people listed as household members. Age was measured as the exact number of years given by the respondent as his or her age. Sex was measured as male or female depending upon how the respondent filled the relevant box asking for this information. Marital status was determined by which of the following categories was circled by the respondent: "married," "divorced," "widowed," "separated," and "single."

Respondents were asked "which of these broad categories describes your total family income before taxes, in 1976?" Income was categorized as: "Less than $5,000," "$5,000 to $9,999," "$10,000 to $14,999," "$15,000 to $19,999," "$20,000 to $24,999," "$25,000 to $34,999," "$35,000 to $49,999," and "$50,000 or more." Respondents were also asked to indicate "The highest level of education you have completed" from the following categories: "No formal education," "Grade school," "Some high school," "High school graduate," "Some college," "College graduate," "Some graduate work," and "A graduate degree." The occupation variable is based upon the occupation of the respondent if he was male; if respondent was female then husband's occupation is used; if female respondent had no husband then her occupation is used. Respondents were asked to list the title of their "usual occupation" and the usual occupation of their spouse or living partner.

The precise manner in which responses to the above demographic questions are categorized for analyses will be indicated as needed. Responses obtained only from the person who answered the questionnaire are used in the analyses (except in some instances regarding occupation), even though personal information was collected on the spouse or living partner of the respondent as well. Since 53.7 percent of the respondents are male and 43.0 percent are female (3.3 percent did not indicate their sex), both sexes are adequately represented in the responses which comprise the data for analysis.

RECAPITULATION AND DISCUSSION

Current knowledge of American housing preferences is scanty at best. Few studies have examined housing preferences in the past, and those that have suffer from sampling problems as well as an expression of preferences based on a limited range of housing choices. In terms of understanding American housing preferences, deriving policy strategies to adequately house families, and predicting the housing situations in which future generations will live, available housing preference information is inadequate.

Two major trends operating in American society demand a more complete understanding of housing preferences. First, rising housing prices which are outpacing people's incomes, along with high mortgage interest rates, are eliminating many families from their preferred housing market. Second, changes in the availability of some housing resources such as land in desirable residential locations and reasonably priced energy to heat and cool homes indicate a long range problem regarding substantial numbers of Americans purchasing conventional single family detached homes placed on private lots. Other important reasons for studying housing preferences include the strong influence that housing exerts on perceived quality of life, the possibility of utilizing housing preference information in formulating public policy, and the predisposition for people to act on their housing preferences.

In an effort to reach a better understanding of housing preferences a mail survey was conducted in Washington State which does not suffer from the problems of past research studies. Responses from this survey provide valuable knowledge of housing preferences, and serve as the basis for the remainder of this book.

3

Prediction of Housing Preferences from Knowledge of Housing Norms

In the United States certain norms prescribe the kinds of housing situations in which people ought to live. Separate norms have developed which encourage people to live in housing which entails ownership, is a single family detached dwelling, has private outside space, and is built in a conventional fashion. What this implies is that ownership of a detached single family home should be the preferred American housing situation.

The present chapter examines these four housing norms and the way in which they influence housing preferences. Our discussion of the housing norms will be based on two expectations, or hypotheses. First, we hypothesize: *housing situations will be preferred to a greater or lesser extent depending on how closely they satisfy the four housing norms.* If this expectation receives substantial support, it allows us to determine the extent to which any housing situation will be considered desirable by Americans.

The second expectation concerns an extremely pressing question in an era characterized by rapid fluctuations in the housing market. Specifically, if people cannot attain their first housing preference, how do they select a reasonable alternative? We hypothesize: *if the most preferred housing situation is not attainable, people will substitute a housing situation which most closely satisfies a similar number and similar kinds of norms as met by their first preference.*

Before these two hypotheses can be evaluated, it is necessary to arrive at a clear conception of American housing norms.

AMERICAN HOUSING NORMS

The concept of norms is central to the study of social behavior and human society. Sumner (1906) first came to grips with the concept over 75 years ago when he classified norms based on a continuum ranging from folkways to mores. Since that time the concept of norms has been subjected to further clarification and has provided the basis of several typological schemes (Gibbs, 1978). Of the numerous definitions of norms, the following four have received a considerable degree of acceptance among social scientists:

1. Norms are generally accepted, sanctioned prescriptions for, or prohibitions against, others' behavior, belief, or feeling; i.e., what others ought to do, believe, feel--or else (Morris, 1956:610).

2. A norm, then, is a rule or a standard that governs our conduct in the social situations in which we participate. It is a societal expectation. It is a standard to which we are expected to conform whether we actually do so or not (Bierstedt, 1963:222).

3. (A norm designates) any standard or rule that states what human beings should or should not think, say, or do under given circumstances (Black and Davis, 1964:456).

4. A norm . . . involves: (1) a collective evaluation in terms of what ought to be; (2) a collective expectation as to what behavior will be; and/or (3) particular reactions to behavior, including attempts to apply sanctions or otherwise induce a particular kind of conduct (Gibbs, 1965:589).

Given the above definitions of norms, it can be concluded that norms are shared rules or guidelines that prescribe the behavior that is appropriate in a given situation. Thus, following Gibbs' definitional attributes of norms, societal members agree to a considerable extent on what kind of behavior ought to occur in a particular situation (e.g., home owners ought to maintain lawns in good condition), can predict that such behavior will take place (e.g., if a home owner's lawn is in poor condition, steps will be taken to remedy this situation), and are aware of the sanctions that conformance or nonconformance to the norm bring (e.g., disapproval or approval from neighbors depending upon the lawn's condition).

The vast majority of the literature on norms focuses on expected and/or observed behavior. However, as suggested in the definition proposed by Morris, norms also influence beliefs, attitudes, and feelings. For example, there is a norm in American society against murder. Not only can we predict that people will ordinarily not commit murder, we can predict that people will hold an attitude against murder. This is an important point for the present study as it is concerned with how housing norms influence preferences for particular housing situations.

Norms are a primary means to ensure the smooth functioning of society; therefore, norms have developed around all important situations. Norms thus enable us to predict how others will behave in a particular situation, and know what is expected of ourselves in that same situation. As stated by Freedman (1968:216):

> One of the fundamental principles of sociology is that when many members of a society face a recurrent problem with important social consequences they tend to develop a normative solution for it. This solution, a set of rules for behavior in a particular situation, becomes part of the culture, and the society indoctrinates its members to conform by explicit or implicit rewards or punishments.

A problem that all Americans face throughout their lives and which has important social consequences is obtaining housing. At a basic level, some form of housing is required to protect humans from the hazards of the natural environment. Housing is also needed to provide privacy. The housing environment in which we live also influences the kinds of neighbors, schools, stores, and protection available to us. In addition, people's housing influences how others respond to them. For example, coworkers would probably react positively toward you if you invite them to a party held in a spacious single family home with a large yard. On the other hand, the reaction may be less favorable if the party is held in a small mobile home located in a mobile home park. Thus, it is not surprising that norms have developed which set down expectations for housing behavior.

As suggested by the Freedman quote, members of a society learn the norms of that society through socialization. An individual learns the norms which relate to housing primarily from his or her parents and the mass media. This learning occurs through both direct and indirect methods. For example, a child might be told by his or her parents that a certain family living in a mobile home park is living in the "wrong" part of town. Or, one might hear the President of the United States say on television that home owners are the backbone of American society. In this fashion housing norms become internalized by societal members.

All norms are supported by sanctions. There exist social rewards for conformity to norms and social punishments for non-conformity to norms. The sanctions differ in their severity and consistency. If a family decides to purchase a mobile home located in a mobile home park, possible sanctions range from not receiving favorable mortgage terms from the bank (severe negative sanction) to disapproving nods from friends (mild nega-tive sanction). On the other hand, if a family decides to pur-chase a single family detached dwelling, sanctions range from receiving favorable mortgage terms (strong positive sanction) to approving nods from friends (mild positive sanction). In terms of consistency in application, the stronger the norm then the more consistent are the sanctions applied to that norm. If home ownership is a strong housing norm, it will carry consistent sanctions that apply to conformance or nonconformance. Sanctions might be applied haphazardly if the norm is not a strong one.

There is never perfect conformance to a particular norm. As stated by Morris and Winter (1978:23): "For any cultural norm there is an ideal level of conformance and some range of permissible variation around the ideal . . . Outside that range, behavior would be negatively sanctioned." Obviously all Ameri-cans do not live in the same type of housing situation. Thus, some Americans are not conforming to all the housing norms. An example of this idea can be seen regarding home ownership. Typically, American families are expected to own their home. However, some deviation from this norm is allowed. A young family with no children and little equity may not be expected to own their home, and few (if any) negative sanctions are applied to that family. On the other hand, a middle-aged couple with children and equity are expected to own a home, and sanctions are applied to encourage compliance to the norm.

Of course some people are unable to obtain housing which meets cultural standards. Lack of knowledge regarding housing options, low income, the high cost of housing, lack of credit, and racial and ethnic discrimination may prevent some people from obtaining culturally desirable housing (Lindamood and Hanna, 1979:Chapter 3). Although these people may strongly prefer single family home ownership and attempt to obtain this housing situation, their efforts are unsuccessful due to the operation of any or all of the possible constraints.

The final point to be addressed regarding housing norms is that they do not rapidly change over time: "Housing norms must be assumed to be relatively fixed in order to permit study

of their influence on behavior at a specific point in time"
(Morris and Winter, 1978:27). As we shall see, the norm for
home ownership has remained strong since the country's beginning and shows no sign of weakening. However, this is not to
say that norms never change. The fact is that norms can
change over time. For example, a norm for fee-simple ownership (i.e., ownership of a detached dwelling) may change
slightly in response to the increasing costs of home ownership.
Perhaps condominium ownership (i.e., nontraditional ownership
of a multiple family dwelling) may grow in popularity while
fee-simple ownership may lose some popularity.

Now that we have a general notion regarding housing
norms, it is possible to specify four major housing norms that
exist in American society. Although these housing norms have
been suggested by previous researchers, they have never been
explicitly enumerated in one source. Our examination of housing norms will proceed in three stages: general discussion,
support from previous studies relating to housing norms, and
sanctions applied to encourage compliance to and discourage
noncompliance from the norms. These housing norms are met to
varying degrees by the seven housing situations presented to
respondents in this study.

Home Ownership

The first housing norm that can be identified in American
society is home ownership. Home ownership has been favored
over renting one's dwelling since the nation's founding. Indeed, a major attraction which drew settlers to the North American continent was the opportunity to own a home (Wedin, 1979:
17). Presently, 65 percent of Americans live in a home which
they own or are buying (U.S. Bureau of the Census, 1979),
with many more expressing a desire for home ownership. The
strength of this norm has been aptly captured by Abrams
(1946:36):

> Home ownership is America's tradition. American
> poets have sung its praises. Our chief executives
> have proclaimed it as a vital link in democracy. Any
> congressman can deliver a homily on the subject with-
> out a minute's preparation and often does.

Home ownership is one of the most deeply imbedded norms
in our society and is well documented. Those researchers finding a majority of people stating a desire for owning a home include Caplow (1948), Hinshaw and Allott (1972), Montgomery
and McCabe (1973), Morris and Winter (1976), Rosow (1948),
Rushing (1970), and Williams (1971). Some of these studies

found a vast majority desiring home ownership. For example, both Caplow (1948) and Rosow (1948) reported that approximately 90 percent of their respective study participants expressed a desire for home ownership. Montgomery and McCabe (1973) found in their study that home ownership was the most important reason given for moving. Further, even renters desired to own their home (Rosow, 1948), and frequently moved to satisfy that desire.

As is the case with any norm, there exist sanctions to encourage conformity to the norm of home ownership. One sanction consists of the federal income tax laws that make interest on mortgage payments and property tax payments to be tax deductible. It has been estimated that home owners saved $9.3 billion from mortgage interest deductions and $6.6 billion from property tax deductions in 1978 (U.S. News and World Report, 1979:64), with these savings estimated to increase to $27.9 billion and $9.5 billion, respectively, in 1984 (U.S. News and World Report, 1983:75). Certainly some people have purchased homes primarily because of the generous tax benefits involved. The availability of government insured mortgages has also encouraged home ownership. The introduction of the amortized, long-term mortgage, often in the form of VA, FHA, and FmHA loans, has provided many Americans the opportunity to buy a home. In short, our entire federal housing policy has been oriented around encouraging, developing, and supporting home ownership (Yearns, 1979:90).

Home ownership has clear advantages over renting with regard to financial benefits, and these advantages serve to encourage home ownership. Cohen and Hansen (1972:266) point out that lending institutions and creditors are more apt to give credit to owners as opposed to renters. The tendency for housing to appreciate in value at a rate greater than the overall cost of living is another incentive to purchase one's home. Yearns (1979) suggests that buying a home is the safest financial investment and hedge against inflation that consumers can make, assuming they live in the home a minimum of three and one-half years. Finally, the money which is employed to pay monthly house payments is a type of "forced savings" that accrues as equity increases. Even though conditions may change in the future (e.g., high interest rates which make it difficult to sell houses) home ownership is likely to remain an important norm.

In contrast, renting has serious drawbacks. The money which is used to pay monthly rent payments is lost to the renter; thus, no equity is built. Renting does not provide a hedge against inflation because money is not invested into the home. Further, renting costs increase along with an increase in the rate of inflation. The income tax advantages for home owners do not apply to renters. Another drawback to renting a home is that the renter is in a subordinate position with regard to a landlord. Finally, renters are limited in the changes they can make in their home. Conversely, owners have a greater degree of freedom to use, maintain, and improve their home. These disadvantages serve to discourage renting one's home and encourage home ownership.

The desire to own one's home is not based solely on economic grounds; rather, it is also based on noneconomic grounds (Branch, 1942; Coons and Glaze, 1963; Rosow, 1948). Some of the noneconomic factors encouraging people to conform to the norm of home ownership are the enhanced prestige, family security, and psychic well-being that home ownership provides. Home owners especially receive positive sanctions via their increased status in the eyes of the community. Further, as stated by Dubos (1968), home ownership is a symbol of both social and economic independence.

Single Family Detached Dwelling

Morris and Winter (1978:111) state that "the basic idea that each family should have its own separate structure with a certain amount of exterior space and relatively clear-cut boundaries has characterized American housing attitudes since the beginning." Cooper (1972) says much the same thing when she describes the ideal American home as a free-standing, square, detached, single family home. This desire for a single family home is borne out by examining the nation's occupied housing stock which reveals that 64 percent of Americans currently live in detached single family homes (U.S. Bureau of the Census, 1978). Thus, the detached single family dwelling is a second housing norm that can be ascertained.

A norm for the detached single family dwelling has been suggested by the findings of several studies, including Belcher (1970), Canter and Thorne (1972), Gerardi (1976), Hinshaw and Allott (1972), Ladd (1972), McCray and Day (1977), McKown (1975), Michelson (1966; 1967), Montgomery and Kivlin (1962), Morris and Winter (1976), Thornburg (1975), and Williams (1971). In fact, this norm is so strong among Americans that Michelson (1966:358) concluded from his research that: "Along one dimension of environment, housing type, there is no variation in the characteristics of people who chose one alternative or another. The popularity of the single family house is so great that its choice is independent of any variable analyzed." Williams (1971:549) found that 94.5 percent of his respondents selected a single family home as their favorite housing structure type, while Gerardi (1976) and the Professional Builder (1975) found close to 90 percent selecting this option. Even among those who presently live in multiple family homes, the single family home is desired by the majority (Lansing, et al., 1964:46-49; Norcross, 1973).

This norm is particularly strong for families with children. Morris and Winter (1978) suggest that the norm is relaxed somewhat for those who are single and for families with no children. However, once there are children there is considerable pressure to live in a single family home. This is particularly true if the children are of school age (Lindamood, 1974). Not only does a single family home often mean more space for family members, it also is usually located near good schools and services for the children.

Although home ownership and occupancy of a detached single family dwelling are highly interrelated (i.e., single family home ownership), living in detached single family dwellings has been encouraged via a multitude of ways in American society which are separate from home ownership incentives. Specifically, the Homestead Act required farmers to live on their own land. Thus, this act prevented the possibility of farmers sharing homes or sharing side-walls of their homes. Zoning ordinances often dictate certain minimum distances between dwellings and prevent the construction of attached structures in many desirable locations within a community. For example, in most suburban areas there is a prohibition against multiple family dwellings and mobile homes. Further, such zoning ordinances, in conjunction with building codes, often mandate the construction of detached structures for reasons of health and fire protection.

There are two major economic incentives for living in a single family home. Since being a home owner means largely to own a single family home, the same tax breaks for ownership apply to most of those who live in single family homes. Secondly, and perhaps more importantly, the resale value for single family homes is higher than that for other structure types with similar features (Angell, 1979:264).

A single family detached dwelling is encouraged by noneconomic incentives as well. Specifically, the single family home is accorded the most prestige of the various structure types. Cooper (1972:173) states that the single family home is the only structure type "in which the self and the family unit can be seen as separate, unique, private and protected." Conversely, the images of the apartment and mobile home are rejected as home, for a home can only be seen as "a free-standing house-on-the-ground" (Cooper, 1972:172). Other advantages of the

apartment is not home,

single family home, as contrasted with other structure types, are acoustical and visual privacy, unrestricted use of immediate exterior areas, larger inside space, and the ability to have pets and children (Angell, 1979).

Private Outside Space

A third housing norm that can be identified is private outside space. Specifically, a home should have private outside space which is continuous with the living indoor space. Traditionally this attribute of housing has been considered an essential component of the detached structure, as indicated by the above statement by Morris and Winter. However, among the housing alternatives currently available to Americans are detached structures with limited (or no) private outside space (e.g., mobile home located in a mobile home park), and attached structures that often provide private outside space (e.g., townhouse and duplex). Thus, the norm for private outside space can be considered as separate from the norm for a detached single family home.

Support for the existence of such a norm is found in studies conducted by Gerardi (1976), Hinshaw and Allott (1972), Ladd (1972), Michelson (1967), and Williams (1971). Hinshaw and Allott (1972:105-106) discovered that their respondents preferred to live in a small house with individual private outside space over a larger house with outside space shared by other families. This finding supports Michelson's (1976:146) suggestion that "public open space, no matter how large, does not allow activities that people want to perform on private space, no matter how small." Similarly, Gerardi (1976) found that among her respondents interest in common areas and shared recreational facilities was low. People desired their own yard. Ladd (1972) found that most of her respondents wanted to live in a house "with a big fence around it . . . a garden and a place where kids can play." Thus, a large private yard was something a vast majority of her study participants desired.

Conformance to the norm of private outside space has been encouraged in a variety of ways. First, the fact that land has been plentiful and relatively inexpensive in the United States has encouraged people to own land. Such a norm does not exist in many denser regions of the world (Barlowe, 1979:61). Second, high prestige is accorded to private outside space. Neighbors' evaluation of a family depends in part on the existence of private outside space, and the quality of that space (e.g., size of the yard, neatness of lawn, and existence of flowers and trees). A significant advantage of having private

outside space is that children can play in close proximity to
their parents, and can be constrained in their activities by a
fence. A yard may also allow the opportunity to own a pet and
to grow a garden. Finally, private outside space allows family
members to lounge in relative privacy.

Conventional Construction

A norm has also developed for the materials from which
dwellings are constructed, and the building process by which
these materials are put together. Conventional construction is
described by Morris and Winter (1978:121) as: "Building a
home piece by piece on the site, as opposed to factory production of mobile homes, modules, or components." Although any
housing structure can be designed and built in an unconventional manner (including single family homes which can be constructed in factories and then set up on building sites in less
than a day), this possibility was not incorporated into the present study (e.g., by asking about modular or sectionalized
homes). Thus, this study is limited to distinguishing between
housing which is typically conventional and housing which is
necessarily constructed in an unconventional manner--namely,
mobile homes. Not only are mobile homes built in factories and
then transported to a predetermined site location, but the materials from which they are constructed and their recognizable
rectangular shape also exhibit an unconventional quality.

Unfortunately, there has been no research conducted
which directly measures the norm of conventional structure.
However, some indirect evidence does exist. Muessig (1979)
has pointed out that housing is one industry which has not
been greatly affected by the industrial revolution. The fact
that housing construction remains largely an on-site process reflects the strength of this norm. Unconventional homes remain
unpopular among most Americans because they bring forth the
image of mass-produced repetitious houses. This notion runs
counter to people's desire to live in a home which reflects their
individuality. Further, many Americans value the sense of security and continuity symbolized by traditional materials and
styles (Muessig, 1979).

With regard to actual living conditions, the majority of
Americans live in conventionally constructed homes. Of the
housing units produced in the United States during 1979,
approximately 61 percent were conventionally site-built homes,
14 percent were mobile homes, and the remaining 25 percent
were prefabricated or modular homes (Automation in Housing,
1980:20). Attempts to popularize unconventional housing have

typically met with failure (e.g., Operation Breakthrough sponsored by HUD). However, mobile homes are one type of unconventional housing that has received some degree of support.

When the mobile home is considered in some detail, one realizes that its unconventional nature is reinforced in many ways. Mobile homes are usually relegated to the less desirable locations within a community. There exists a limited range of financing terms for those who want to purchase a mobile home, which typically carry higher interest rates and have less protection against foreclosure and repossession. Mobile homes are also more susceptible to wind and fire threats. For example, the incidence of mobile home wind destruction was over 500 percent greater than that for single family homes between 1970 and 1977 (Angell, 1979). Residents of mobile homes are more apt to have conflicts with their landlords. Further, a major drawback of mobile homes is that they do not appreciate at quite the same rate as do single family homes; thus, they are considered as second-rate financial investments. In fact, mobile homes have often depreciated in value. Finally, mobile homes are frowned upon by most Americans, as they violate the true image of a home. As Cooper (1972:175) states: "A person who lives in a house that moves must somehow be as unstable as the structure he inhabits." Thus, there exist effective sanctions to encourage Americans to live in conventionally constructed housing.

Relative Strength of the Housing Norms

A question which might be raised at this juncture is: Which of the four housing norms is the strongest in American society? Unfortunately, no definitive answer can be given in response to this question. There has been no research in which the relative strength of the four housing norms has been directly examined. Further, any indirect evidence that does exist is weak and inconclusive. One method which can be followed to obtain a general idea concerning the strength of housing norms is to tabulate the number of times each norm has been supported in past empirical research. Table 3 shows the number of times each norm has been supported in the 17 studies that have been previously discussed in relation to norms. The table reveals that single family detached dwelling (13) was mentioned most often as being supported by study participants, followed by ownership (7) and private outside space (5). The norm for conventional structure was not addressed in any of these studies. Based on these findings, we might conclude that housing norms vary in strength in the following manner: single family detached dwelling, ownership, private outside space, and conventional structure.

Table 3. Housing Norms Revealed in Previous Research

Study	Housing Norms			
	Ownership	Detached Dwelling	Private Outside Space	Conventional Construction
Hinshaw and Allott (1972)	X	X	X	
Montgomery and McCabe (1973)	X			
Morris and Winter (1976)	X	X		
Michelson (1966)		X		
Michelson (1967)		X	X	
McCray and Day (1977)		X		
Williams (1971)	X	X	X	
Montgomery and Kivlin (1962)		X		
Caplow (1948)	X			
Rosow (1948)	X			
Ladd (1972)		X	X	
Rushing (1970)	X			
McKown (1975)		X		
Canter and Thorne (1972)		X		
Belcher (1970)		X		
Thornburg (1975)		X		
Gerardi (1976)		X	X	

NOTE: An X indicates that the relevant study revealed support for the norm.

However, other researchers have proposed that home own-ership is the strongest held norm. Angell (1979:248) points out that recent trends in the housing industry indicate that owner-ship is more important to Americans than is a single family de-tached dwelling. When consumers are forced to choose between ownership and single family detached dwelling, they usually se-lect ownership. This may well be a factor in the growing number of Americans who are purchasing (primarily through condominium ownership) townhouses, duplexes, and apartments. Thus, it appears that the structure type norm is compromised first. No such comparative evidence exists with regard to the other housing norms.

Given the above conflicting results and the absence of any real conclusive data, we will not attempt to rank the norms in terms of their strength. Rather, we will consider each of the housing norms as being equally important to Americans, al-though some qualifying remarks may be made at appropriate points in the text. Clearly, the measurement of how strongly Americans hold each of the housing norms is a crucial topic for future research.

Figure 1 indicates the extent to which each of the seven housing situations presented to respondents in this study meets the four general housing norms just described. In the figure, one point is assigned if a housing situation completely satisfies a particular norm, while one-half a point is assigned if it is questionable whether a housing situation satisfies a particular norm (e.g., in some cases a townhouse has private outside space while in other cases it does not). No point is assigned if the housing situation clearly does not satisfy a particular hous-ing norm.

The figure shows that substantial variation exists in the compliance of the housing situations to the four norms, ranging from single family home ownership which meets all four norms to renting an apartment which meets only one norm. Tentatively, we might expect that the extent to which each of the housing situations satisfies these norms will be in direct correlation to the degree that a particular choice is preferred by respon-dents. We would therefore expect that single family home own-ership will be preferred to a greater extent than the six alternative choices. The alternative choices will be preferred in the following order: own mobile home and lot, rent single fam-ily home, own townhouse, rent duplex, own mobile home on rented space, and rent apartment. Thus, the housing situations addressed in the present study will vary in the strength of preference directed at them according to the num-ber of norms they satisfy.

TYPES OF NORMS	BUY SINGLE FAMILY HOUSE	BUY MOBILE HOME AND LOT	RENT SINGLE FAMILY HOUSE	BUY TOWNHOUSE	RENT DUPLEX	BUY MOBILE HOME ON RENTED SPACE	RENT APARTMENT
OWNERSHIP	★	★		★		☆	
PRIVATE OUTSIDE SPACE	★	★	★	☆	☆		
CONVENTIONAL STRUCTURE	★		★	★	★		★
DETACHED STRUCTURE	★	★	★			★	
NUMBER OF NORMS SATISFIED	4	3	3	2½	1½	1½	1

Figure 1.   General Norms Satisfied by the Seven Housing Situations under Study

Note: Filled star indicates norm is fully satisfied, while hollow star indicates that this norm is sometimes satisfied.

We might also expect that if people are unable to attain their most preferred housing situation, they will select a substitute in a rational and predictable manner. Specifically, the first housing preference satisfies a certain number of norms as well as particular kinds of norms. It seems reasonable to expect that the second housing preference would satisfy a very similar number and similar kinds of norms as met by the most preferred housing situation. Thus, if people cannot purchase a single family home, their second choice would most likely be owning a mobile home (where conventional structure type is lost) or renting a single family home (where ownership is lost).

THE MOST PREFERRED HOUSING SITUATION

We first turn our attention to the question: Is a particular housing situation preferred to a greater extent as the number of norms it satisfies increases? The percentage of respondents who selected each housing situation as their first preference is shown in the first column of Table 4. Overwhelmingly, single family home ownership was the most preferred housing option; three-quarters of the respondents selected it as their first preference. Interest in all other possibilities was relatively low, with the number two choice of owning a mobile home and lot being selected by only 7.6 percent of the respondents. The remaining five housing situations were preferred by between 4.7 percent and 2.6 percent of the respondents. When all of the alternative housing situations (i.e., not entailing single family home ownership) are considered as a whole, it is discovered that only one-quarter of the respondents selected any of them as their first preference.

The second column of Table 4 shows respondents' second preference, i.e., what housing situation would be preferred if for some reason their first preference could not be fulfilled. From a policy standpoint this is perhaps the more interesting of the preference questions, as it suggests the adaptation people are likely to seek if single family home ownership becomes increasingly difficult to obtain. Given our discussion of rising housing costs and growing scarcity of crucial building resources, it is probable that many Americans will be faced with the possibility of living in their second preferred housing situation in the future.

There are three housing environments which received substantial support as respondents' second preference: owning a mobile home and lot (27.2 percent), renting a single family home (20.3 percent), and owning a townhouse (17.9 percent). The remaining four choices were each selected by less than

Table 4. Housing Situations Which People Prefer (Percent)

Choices	First Preference	Second Preference	Combined First and Second Preference	Number of Housing Norms Satisfied
	N = 2655			
Buy single family house	76.2	6.8	83.0	4
Buy mobile home and lot	7.6	27.2	34.8	3
Rent single family house	3.1	20.3	23.4	3
Buy townhouse	2.9	17.9	20.8	2½
Rent duplex	2.6	9.6	12.2	1½
Rent apartment	4.7	6.1	10.8	1
Buy mobile home on rented space	2.9	4.6	7.5	1½
Gave first preference but no second preference	--	7.5	7.5	--
Total	100.0	100.0	200.0	

10 percent of the respondents. Obviously the small percentage of respondents selecting single family home ownership as their second preference is an outcome of its overwhelming choice as the number one preference. The housing situation which received the lowest amount of support was owning a mobile home on rented space (4.6 percent). Thus, some of the viable housing alternatives in which people could live do not receive a great deal of support.

Finally, Table 4 presents the combined percentage of respondents who selected each housing situation as their first or second preference. Owning a single family home was preferred by the largest percentage of respondents (83.0 percent from a possible 200 percent), while owning a mobile home on rented space was preferred by the smallest percentage of respondents (7.5 percent). The rank order of combined first and second preference is strikingly consistent with the hypothesis that a housing situation will be preferred to a greater extent as the number of norms it satisfies increases. This can be seen by comparing the combined first and second preference percentages (third column) with the number of norms satisfied by each housing situation (fourth column) in Table 4. The only reversal of the predicted pattern occurs between renting an apartment (10.8 percent) and owning a mobile home on rented space (7.5 percent); the former is judged to satisfy one of the housing norms while the latter meets one and a half norms. It should also be noted that there is a considerable percentage difference between those respondents who preferred owning a mobile home and lot (34.8 percent) and those who preferred renting a single family home (23.4 percent), although both housing situations satisfy three of the norms. This difference suggests that the norm for home ownership may be more important to people than is the norm for single family detached dwelling.

Evidence From Another Question

The results of another preference question asked of respondents--namely, to what extent would respondents consider each housing situation--provides additional information. This question should produce slightly different results than that found by the previous two questions. Whereas respondents were forced to select only one housing situation as their first preference and then a second housing situation as their second preference, this question asked respondents to evaluate each housing situation one at a time. Thus, we have data revealing the extent respondents considered each of the seven housing situations. The findings are reported in Table 5.

Table 5. Extent to Which Alternative Housing Situations Would be Considered (Percent)

Choices	Consider Choice?					Mean	S.D.
	Definitely No	Probably No	Unsure	Probably Yes	Definitely Yes		
Buy single family house	10.3	5.1	7.9	33.9	42.8	3.94	1.28
Buy mobile home and lot	53.9	17.2	11.8	12.8	4.2	1.96	1.24
Rent single family house	52.3	20.2	11.6	13.7	2.2	1.93	1.18
Rent duplex	53.4	20.6	13.7	10.8	1.5	1.86	1.11
Rent apartment	64.7	16.0	8.2	9.4	1.7	1.68	1.08
Buy townhouse	59.9	20.5	10.4	8.1	1.1	1.70	1.02
Buy mobile home on rented space	74.9	13.3	5.5	5.3	1.0	1.44	.89

Perhaps the best way to interpret Table 5 is by adding the percentage of respondents who said they would either probably or definitely consider a particular housing situation. Once again, single family home ownership (76.7 percent) was the clearly preferred housing situation. Owning a mobile home and lot (17.0 percent) and renting a single family home (15.9 percent) were, respectively, the number two and three most preferred housing environments. These results are also consistent with those presented in Table 4; however, the percentage difference between these two housing situations is not nearly as large as that found in Table 4. Both housing situations satisfy an identical number of norms so this small percentage difference is closer to what might be expected.

The next three most preferred housing situations do not perfectly conform to the ranking predicted by the hypothesis that a housing situation will be preferred to a greater extent as the norms it satisfies increases. Renting a duplex (12.3 percent) was ranked fourth instead of fifth, renting an apartment (11.1 percent) was ranked fifth instead of seventh, and owning a townhouse (9.2 percent) was ranked sixth instead of fourth. However, the percentage differences between these three housing situations are not large ones, the largest percentage difference being 3.1 percent. Finally, owning a mobile home on rented space (6.3 percent) was the least preferred choice, matching the result found in Table 4.

Conclusion

Based on the data presented in the above two tables, considerable support is given to our initial expectation that as the number of norms satisfied by a housing situation increases, the level of preference directed at that housing situation increases. This hypothesis is particularly supported in terms of the overwhelming preference for single family home ownership, the only housing situation which satisfies all four norms. The level of preference given for owning a mobile home and lot and renting a single family home, both of which meet three norms, also support the hypothesis, especially the results presented in Table 5.

When we consider housing situations which are generally not very popular among the respondents, then the hypothesis is not supported to such a great extent. This finding may be the result of several factors. First, the housing norms may be given unequal weight by respondents. As mentioned previously, ownership may be a stronger norm than the other three norms. Actually, private outside space may be the most important norm. Our data show that the three most popular housing situations all involve private outside space, while the bottom four housing situations do not always involve it. However, there is no legitimate basis now available to decide how to rank the norms with regard to their strength. For the time being we must simply regard this as a distinct possibility.

Second, some of the housing situations receiving weak support may be unfamiliar to respondents. Thus, options such as renting a duplex or owning a townhouse are relative unknowns to many Americans. If this is indeed the case, respondents may not realize what norms are satisfied by a particular housing situation. For example, people may not realize that owning a townhouse can entail private outside space, and thus they give it less support than it might normally receive. If, in the future, a growing number of Americans are forced to seriously consider the alternatives to single family home ownership, it might be predicted that knowledge about each alternative will increase. As a result, we might expect the level of preference directed at each housing situation to conform more closely to the predicted pattern.

Finally, it is possible that many Americans do not even consider any housing situation except for single family home ownership, or a housing situation which comes very close to meeting the norms satisfied by single family home ownership (i.e., renting a single family home and owning a mobile home and lot). If at least two norms are no longer satisfied by a particular housing environment, most people may not regard it as a viable possibility. Thus, the responses given for the four least preferred choices may not have been considered carefully by respondents. For this reason, the results presented in Table 4 are probably more accurate than those presented in Table 5. It is probably easier for respondents to select their top two preferences than it is to critically evaluate each possible housing situation, particularly since some options are unfamiliar and others are regarded as clearly inferior.

IF THE FIRST PREFERENCE CANNOT BE ACHIEVED

When faced with the necessity of selecting a less desirable housing situation than their first preference, what choices are people willing to make? Earlier it was hypothesized that people's second choice will satisfy a similar number and similar kinds of norms as their first choice. We will now test this hypothesis by examining the data provided by the three preference questions: most preferred housing situation, second most preferred housing situation, and extent to which each housing situation would be considered. Table 6 displays the relationship between the responses obtained from the first two preference questions.

One important finding in Table 6 is displayed in the first row. Since it is single family home ownership that meets all four housing norms and is therefore the most preferred housing situation, and also the option most threatened by inflation and resource scarcity, it is particularly crucial to assess what alternatives would be acceptable to those who may be unable to attain their preference for single family home ownership. The respondents who selected owning a single family home as their first preference differed greatly in their second preference, as three alternatives emerged: owning a mobile home and lot (35.8 percent), renting a single family home (26.4 percent), and owning a townhouse (23.5 percent). The remaining alternatives were selected by only 7.0 percent to 2.7 percent of these respondents. Thus, although there was no single second preference that was dominant among those preferring single family home ownership, some choices were clearly perceived as more desirable than others.

Table 6 also reveals that regardless of respondents' first choice, they tended to choose a second preference that was close to their first preference in terms of the number of norms satisfied by those housing environments. For example, in no instance did 20 percent or more of those with a given first preference give as a second preference a housing situation that differed from the first preference by more than one and one-half in the number of norms it satisfied. For example, very few of those who selected renting an apartment as their first preference (which meets one norm) gave as a second choice single family home ownership, owning a mobile home and lot, or renting a single family home, housing environments which meet most or all of the norms. Conversely, those whose first preference was single family home ownership steered away from the options of renting a duplex, renting an apartment, or owning a mobile home on rented space as their second choice. Clearly, people's second housing preferences exhibited a discernible similarity to their most desired housing situation, as predicted by the second housing norm hypothesis. This finding suggests that although single family home ownership is clearly the most preferred choice of a majority of people, there exists a minority who do not perceive this housing situation as a viable option. Specifically, the minority of respondents selecting housing situations not conforming to most of the norms as their first preference, continued to avoid single family home ownership (as indicated by their second preference) in what appears to be an understandable manner.

Table 6. Relationship between First and Second Housing Preference (Percent)

First Preference	N	Second Preference[c]						
		Buy Single Family House	Buy Mobile Home and Lot	Rent Single Family House	Buy Townhouse	Rent Duplex	Rent Apartment	Buy Mobile Home on Rented Space
Buy single family house	(1868)	--[a]	35.8 (1)	26.4 (1)	23.5 (1½)	7.0	4.6	2.7
Buy mobile home and lot	(184)	47.3 (1)[b]	--	8.2	4.9	7.6	4.3	27.7 (1½)
Rent single family house	(76)	23.7 (1)	14.5	--	7.9	42.1 (1½)	9.2	2.6
Buy townhouse	(73)	45.2 (1½)	9.6	4.1	--	11.0	26.0 (1½)	4.1
Rent duplex	(60)	8.3	8.3	25.0 (1½)	10.0	--	40.0 (½)	8.3
Rent apartment	(102)	9.8	3.9	6.9	11.8	59.8 (½)	--	7.8
Buy mobile home on rented space	(65)	16.9	36.9 (1½)	9.2	3.1	13.8	20.0 (½)	--

[a] Those who gave the same housing situation as both their first and second preference are excluded from the analysis (n = 15).

[b] Number in parentheses is the difference between number of norms satisfied by most preferred housing situation and number of norms satisfied by second most preferred housing situation. This information is presented only when second preference is stated by 20 percent or more of respondents indicating a particular housing situation as their first preference.

[c] Chi Square = 1712.99, p .001.

The tendency for second preferences to be selected by respondents according to similarity to their most preferred housing situation can be seen more clearly in Figure 2, a graphical
representation of the data presented in Table 6. The area of
each circle drawn in Figure 2 corresponds to the percentage of
respondents choosing the designated option as their first or
second preference. The arrows indicate the percentage of respondents selecting a given housing environment as their first
choice who selected another housing option as their second
choice. Arrows point towards the second housing preference,
and are shown only if at least 20 percent of those preferring
one housing situation gave another as their second preference.
The tendency of respondents to pick as their second preference
a housing situation which was similar to their most desired
housing situation is evident by the clustering of rental options,
multiunit options, and mobile home options.

Respondents simply did not, at least in substantial numbers, select a housing situation as their second preference
which satisfied quite different types of norms as their stated
first preference. Rather, the similarity between first and
second preferences with regard to the types and number of
norms satisfied is strikingly consistent with the prediction made
by the second housing norm hypothesis.

When attention is directed at our second set of data,
extent to which each housing situation is considered, further
support is given for the hypothesis. Table 7 presents a correlation matrix containing all seven housing options and indicates
the direction and statistical significance of the correlations. By
examining the intercorrelations between housing preferences we
can determine the extent to which people who are amenable to
considering one housing situation are amenable to other housing
situations. To a certain extent we can locate housing situations
that people consider viable alternatives if their most preferred
choice is not available. Thus, the same general question addressed in Table 6 can be addressed by the results of this
housing preference question.

In first examining Table 7, it is apparent that the correlations are of such magnitude that all but one are statistically
significant. Some relationships between housing situations are
quite high, while some others are rather low. Generally, it appears that housing preferences cluster into three groups which
lend support to our hypothesis. There is a definite mobile
home grouping ($r = .487$), suggesting that the few who would
consider one mobile home alternative tend to be the ones who
might consider the other choice. The difference in norms met
by the two mobile home alternatives is one and one-half. The
single family home ownership choice appears to stand by itself,

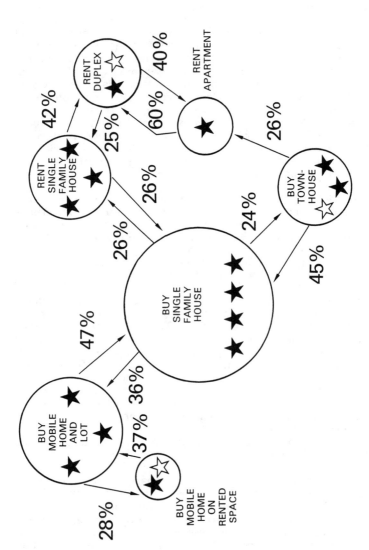

Figure 2.   Percent of Respondents Choosing a Particular First Preference who Choose Other
Alternatives as Second Preference

Note: Arrows point towards second preferences.

as correlations between it and the other housing choices are relatively low (r's between single family home ownership and the other choices range from -.286 to .149). The highest positive correlations are with renting a single family home (r = .149) and owning a townhouse (r = .125). Finally, the four remaining housing situations appear to fit loosely together (r's between these four choices range from .230 to .562). If people prefer a housing situation entailing rent and/or multiunit structure type, they tend to be amenable to similar alternative housing environments. In fact, the highest correlation in the table exists between preferences for renting an apartment and renting a duplex (r = .562), housing situations meeting a nearly identical number of norms.

Thus, based on the data presented in the above table, there appear to be three subgroups in the housing market. These subgroups prefer similar kinds and a similar number of norms to be satisfied by the housing situations in which they would consider living. These findings relate nicely to those obtained from the first two preference questions. In short, the data presented here strongly support the second housing norm hypothesis. If forced to choose a housing situation which is not their most preferred choice, people select as an alternative a housing situation satisfying very similar kinds of norms and approximately the same number of norms. Discrepancies from the predicted pattern may result from the same factors referred to in the discussion of the first housing norm hypothesis-- namely, our inability to measure the strength of the norms, respondents' unfamiliarity with some housing situations, and the possibility that many Americans only consider single family home ownership as a viable housing situation.

RECAPITULATION AND DISCUSSION

Four major housing norms have developed in the United States that prescribe the kinds of housing situations in which people ought to live: home ownership, single family detached dwelling, private outside space, and conventional structure type. Each of the four norms is supported by sanctions which encourage conformity and discourage nonconformity. These sanctions can be quite severe and are relatively consistently applied.

The general question addressed by this chapter was: What effects do housing norms have on housing preferences? To address this question, we examined two hypotheses. The first hypothesis states that a housing situation will be preferred to a greater extent as the number of norms it satisfies

Table 7. Correlation Matrix of Dependent Variables

		Housing Preferences					
Housing Preferences	Buy Single Family House	Buy Mobile Home and Lot	Rent Single Family House	Rent Duplex	Rent Apartment	Buy Townhouse	Buy Mobile Home on Rented Space
Buy single family house	--	-.089*	.149*	-.070*	-.286*	.125*	-.178*
Buy mobile home and lot		--	.114*	.056	-.002	-.034	.487*
Rent single family house			--	.463*	.259*	.230*	.093*
Rent duplex				--	.562*	.340*	.170*
Rent apartment					--	.256*	.171*
Buy townhouse						--	.083*
Buy mobile home on rented space							--

* Significant at .001 level.

increases. It was generally supported by the results of three preference questions asked of respondents. As predicted by the hypothesis, single family home ownership (four norms) was preferred by a vast majority of respondents. Owning a mobile home and lot and renting a single family home (both satisfying three norms) were the number two and three preferences, respectively. By combining the answers of the first two preference questions, the only reversal in the predicted pattern of preferences occurs between renting an apartment (one norm) and owning a mobile home on rented space (one and one-half norms). The results of the third question indicate that the four least preferred housing situations were preferred out of the predicted order to some extent. Several possible explanations of this finding have been stated earlier. However, we conclude that it is possible to predict levels of preference directed at particular housing situations based on the number of norms satisfied by those housing situations.

The second hypothesis states that if people's most preferred housing situation is not attainable for some reason, their second preference will be similar in terms of the number and kinds of housing norms satisfied by the more preferred housing situation. This hypothesis is strongly supported by the results of the three housing preference questions asked of respondents. It was found that the first and second preference rarely differed by more than one and one-half norms. Thus, if people prefer single family home ownership, their second choice is usually a housing situation meeting approximately the same number and kinds of norms. Similarly, those people who prefer a housing situation meeting few norms usually select a similar housing situation as their second preference. Upon closer analysis, it appears that there are three subgroups in the housing market. Some people only consider single family home ownership, others opt for one of the mobile home options, and the remainder tend to select one of the rent and/or multiple family home options. These subgroups tend to select housing situations which have a similar number and similar kinds of housing norms.

In conclusion, it is possible to accurately predict housing preferences based upon knowledge of housing norms. We can predict people's first housing preference fairly accurately by knowing how many norms are met by the various housing situations. If people's first preference is blocked, we can predict their second most preferred housing situation by comparing the various housing options according to the number and kinds of housing norms satisfied. This information seems important in predicting the kinds of homes in which Americans will live in the future.

4

Differences in People's Housing Preferences

Are American housing norms shared equally by everyone or held more strongly by some people than by others? Do such important personal characteristics as education and wealth tend to divide the population or have no effect on the way norms become translated into preferences? In this chapter we attempt to more fully explain housing preferences by assessing the extent to which a series of personal characteristics influence them.

An examination of the relationships between housing preferences and personal characteristics is important because it can shed light on variations in housing preferences between different segments of the population. If we discover that segments of the population differ in their housing preferences, this finding would have significant implications for policy and research. For example, if large families prefer single family home ownership to a greater extent than small families, while the reverse is true for renting an apartment, different housing efforts might be needed to provide large families and small families with appropriate housing. Knowledge of what kinds of people prefer certain types of housing situations would allow policymakers to target segments of the population for specific assistance, thereby obtaining a reasonable match between people and their housing.

Future housing preference research would be more effective if based on knowledge of the housing preferences-personal characteristics relationships. For example, we might find that age and income are the major influential factors in preferences toward mobile homes, while education and marital status are the most important variables explaining preferences toward single family homes. Such discoveries would allow us to focus on the most relevant personal characteristics in conducting housing preference research.

Finally, the following analysis will attempt to resolve two competing viewpoints about how these personal characteristics relate to housing preferences. Derived from a mass society perspective, these viewpoints may be called the "consensus" hypothesis and the "differential" hypothesis.

COMPETING THEORETICAL PERSPECTIVES

A major debate has existed within the field of sociology about the concept of "mass society." The debate revolves around the question of "whether American society is based on a common value system or a class-differential value system" (Han, 1969:679). There has been considerable research supporting both positions, and at the present time neither view has received complete acceptance. Researchers such as Fave (1974), Hamilton (1966), Hyman (1963), Miller (1958), and Tallman and Morgner (1970) have reported that classes differ with regard to subjective variables such as attitudes, values, and aspirations on a variety of matters. Conversely, researchers such as Cloward and Ohlin (1960), Fischer (1975), Han (1969), Merton (1957), Reiss (1963), and Rodman (1963) suggest that American culture is marked by a central-societal emphasis on some commonly shared values such as success.

There are compelling reasons for acceptance of both views. On the one hand, even a casual observer recognizes that American society, like all societies, consists of a diverse group of people, differing with regard to marital status, racial-ethnic background, residence, social class, and a variety of other characteristics. If Americans are so different from one another, it might be expected that they differ in the values and attitudes that they hold. Some scholars have proposed that the various classes are very much different from one another. For example, Miller (1958:6) states that: "There is a substantial segment of present-day American society whose way of life, values, and characteristic patterns of behavior are the product of a distinctive cultural system which may be termed 'lower class.'" In a similar vein, Davis (1946:104) writes that individuals of different classes are "reacting to different realistic situations. . . . Therefore their values and their social goals are different." Thus, the class-differential value hypothesis posits that there are subjective differences between different groups of Americans, particularly based on social class.

On the other hand, it often appears that Americans share certain values, attitudes, and aspirations (Williams, 1959). For example, the success goal has been found to transcend class boundaries (Merton, 1957). The very definition of society infers the widespread acceptance of certain dominant ideas by societal members. Parsons (1959:8) assumes that a common value system underlies society in his reference to "a single more or less integrated system of values" in any society. Merton (1957:141) has made the same assumption: "It is . . . only because behavior is typically oriented toward the basic values of the society that we speak of a human aggregate as comprising a society." It also appears that most Americans strive for a life style characteristic of the middle class. For example, Rushing (1970) points out that most Americans strive for home ownership because it is an important component of the middle class way of life. Further, American life has become increasingly dominated by urban areas, resulting in a leveling off of value differences (Fischer, 1975; Shils, 1963). The trend toward mass education and mass media are representative of, and in turn have contributed to, the reduction of any value differences that may have existed in the past. The majority of Americans are now exposed to the dominant values, attitudes, and aspirations of American culture and internalize them as their own. Thus, there is a common value system in American society. If we accept this view, we would expect few differences to exist among various groups of Americans with regard to subjective notions.

These two competing views can be employed in an attempt to explain housing preferences. In doing so, however, we need to modify their original scope to some extent. As reflected in the above discussion, the majority of research conducted on the mass society concept has entailed analyses of value differences or similarities (such as the value for success) between the social classes (usually measured by either family income or occupational prestige). We believe that past research, and thus the two views regarding the viability of the mass society concept, has been too narrowly focused for two reasons.

First, there is reason to expect value differences based on personal characteristics other than social class, as people differ in a number of ways. It may well be the case that value differences exist according to distinguishing personal characteristics such as age, family life cycle, rural-urban residence, family size, and housing situation, as well as social class. Indeed, this has been shown to be true in much social science research. For example, it has been found that residence influences concern for environmental quality (Tremblay and Dunlap, 1978), family life cycle affects institutional participation (Gove, et al., 1973), and age influences satisfaction with life (Rojek, et al., 1975). Thus, to eliminate consideration of personal characteristics besides social class results in an unnecessary limitation of the scope of the mass society concept. We will use this concept in the wider scope which includes a variety of personal characteristics.

Second, there is no reason to focus on values at the expense of other equally important subjective notions such as attitudes, norms, goals, and preferences. In fact, the abstract nature of values means that they are extremely difficult to accurately measure. Perhaps a focus on the more specific forms of values, as reflected in norms and preferences, is a more viable research strategy. Actually, as Rodman (1963:206) points out, tests of the applicability of the mass society concept do not generally distinguish "between values, norms, aspirations, and (desirable) goals." For example, Morris and Winter (1976) have attempted to explain housing norms with the mass society concept, Fave (1974) and Hyman (1963) considered educational preferences, and Han (1969) focused on socioeconomic level of wish and expectation. Thus, it seems legitimate to apply the mass society concept to an understanding of preferences, since the crucial point of the concept is to account for the desirability of particular items.

Based on the above reasoning for modifying the original scope of the mass society concept, we will employ its two competing viewpoints to examine housing preferences. To make it clear that we are focusing on housing preferences and personal characteristics (which include but are not limited to social class), we will label the two viewpoints the *"consensus housing preference hypothesis"* and *"differential housing preference hypothesis."* Personal characteristics associated with current housing location, current housing situation, household composition, and social class will be considered using these two hypotheses.

Differential Preference Hypothesis

McKown (1975:11) states: "The human aspect of housing is of major concern and people, not technology, should be the primary consideration in the planning and use of housing resources." People's preferences for housing are certainly conditions which need to be taken into account. There is reason to believe that housing preferences vary according to the segment of the population under concern. Thus, it is important to discover how these preferences differ if we are to provide housing that people desire. One way in which Americans differ is their housing needs. It might be expected that people differing in terms of current housing location, current housing situation, household composition, and social class face divergent life conditions. As a result, different housing environments are more suitable for particular kinds of people. Actual housing needs, then, might influence housing preferences. For example, if someone's housing needs can be best satisfied by single family home ownership, that housing environment is preferred.

Another possibility for differential housing preferences is that the four housing norms are not equally internalized among all Americans. Perhaps those in the upper social classes, for example, are more apt to have internalized all four housing norms, while those of the lower social classes have not. Thus, housing preferences may vary because personal characteristics influence the degree to which the housing norms are accepted. Further, people may vary with regard to what norms they are willing to give up if required to do so. For example, large households may first part with the detached structure norm. Based on the differential housing preference hypothesis, then, we would predict that housing preferences are influenced by personal characteristics.

The importance of examining the relationship between personal characteristics and housing preferences has been noted by McCray and Day (1977:244), who state: "Housing today is frequently designed without reference to specific families or types of families. Consumers and builders alike make housing decisions without an understanding of the human dimensions that render structures habitable." This view is supported by Hinshaw and Allott (1972:102), who suggest that housing preferences depend on several characteristics, including personal experience, social and economic realities, age, family life cycle, and income level. Hinshaw and Allott (1972:102) further stress that: "Preferential responses must . . . be evaluated in the light of the particular socioeconomic setting of the respondents." Thus, it appears that it is insufficient to merely state what American housing preferences are. It is also necessary to ascertain the characteristics of the people who prefer various housing environments. From this viewpoint individuals are unique and, as a result, housing preferences vary according to their personal characteristics (Angell, 1979; Williams, 1971).

Current housing location might be predicted to influence housing preferences. Housing situations differ in terms of accessibility and affordability depending on rural or urban location. For example, home ownership is higher in rural areas: 72 percent of rural households owned their home in 1975 compared to 61 percent of urban households (Bird and Kampe, 1977:7-8). Thus it is possible that home ownership is preferred to a greater extent by rural as opposed to urban residents. The detached single family home is also more prevalent in rural areas. In 1975, 80 percent of rural households lived in detached single family dwellings compared to 63 percent of urban households (Bird and Kampe, 1977:7-8). Thus, it might be expected that rural location leads to a preference for a single family home. People living in rural areas are also in an environment containing open spaces, which might lead to a preference for a housing situation entailing a large, private yard. Finally, conventionality may not be as important to those living in rural areas. Mobile homes are reasonably popular in rural areas because it is possible to own the land under the home and zoning regulations are not as stringent as those found in urban areas. We might expect, then, that rural residents prefer single family home ownership and mobile home ownership to a greater extent than urban residents. Conversely, urban residents are more likely to prefer multiple family dwellings and housing situations involving tenancy.

Current housing situation might influence housing preferences. First, we might expect that those currently owning their home prefer home ownership more so than those currently renting their home. Second, we might expect people to prefer the housing structure type in which they currently reside to a greater extent than other housing structure types. The basis of these expectations is the notion that people tend to adapt to their present life situations, and to eventually prefer those situations. Thus, people adapt to their current housing situation and learn to prefer it. One reason single family home ownership is preferred to such a large extent is simply because many Americans have never experienced an alternative housing situation for an extensive period of time. However, those people living in mobile homes or multiple family homes learn to appreciate the advantages of those housing structure types, and eventually to prefer them (Canter and Thorne, 1972; Thornburg, 1975). Similarly, people renting their home may prefer that tenure status, while those owning their home learn to prefer home ownership (Caplow, 1948). Thus, housing preferences vary according to experience with housing structure types and housing tenure statuses.

Household composition is an important variable to consider with regard to housing preferences. Size of household creates differential demands on housing, which in turn may lead to the holding of particular housing preferences. Large households place a premium on large inside space, a detached dwelling, and a yard to ensure privacy and minimize noise problems. Thus, we might expect large households to prefer single family homes. On the other hand, small households do not necessarily need the same things as large households, and may prefer housing options involving multiple family homes.

Age is another important household composition variable to consider, for as people move through the life cycle they may need different kinds of housing environments. As Michelson (1976:110) suggests, "different aspects of environments are salient to people in different stages of the life cycle." Young adults might prefer multiple family homes they can rent to minimize responsibility and perhaps to live close to the workplace. Middle-age adults, who probably have children at home, may desire a single family home with outside space, close to community services such as schools. Older adults may prefer to live in apartments or other multiple family dwellings (Golant, 1977). After the children have left home and retirement arrives, it may be desirable to liquidate the responsibilities of caring for a large home and yard which are no longer needed.

It is possible that marital status affects housing preferences. Single households might prefer townhouses, duplexes, or apartments for much the same reasons as those that apply to young adults. In addition, single households may want to have access to a single population, which can be found in many multiple family dwelling complexes. Married couples, on the other hand, probably want a single family home to be near other married people. Further, marriage has connotations of stability. One way to be stable and a "good citizen" is to buy a single family home.

Sex might also influence housing preferences. Females are generally at home more than males, so the housing environment may be more important to them. The privacy, size, and quiet of a single family home may be desirable to females to a greater extent than males.

There are reasons for expecting social class to influence housing preferences. As Montgomery and McCabe (1973) suggest, standard of living as reflected by social class should affect images of desirable housing environments. It may be the case that those with high incomes prefer housing options involving ownership more so than those with lower incomes (Meyerson, et al., 1962). Low income households may adapt their preferences based on their recognized inability to purchase a home. High income families may also prefer single family homes to a greater extent than lower income families so that they can live in desirable suburban neighborhoods.

The second social class variable, education, reflects the internalization of the society's norms. As educational attainment increases, people tend to internalize more of the housing norms. Thus, those with high education should prefer single family home ownership to a greater extent than those with low education. People with little education might be willing to trade some norms in order to obtain housing which seems "appropriate." Thus, low education households might be more apt to prefer a mobile home because it basically satisfies all the norms with the exception of conventionality.

Occupational prestige, the third social class variable, may influence housing preferences. White collar workers are more likely to reside in suburbs containing single family homes; and they are more likely to prefer this housing environment. Blue collar workers often live in poorer sections of the community where mobile homes and multiple family homes are often viewed as acceptable. Further, blue collar workers may be forced to live close to their workplace, requiring that they live in multiple family homes. Thus, blue collar workers may be more likely to prefer mobile homes and multiple family homes as opposed to white collar workers.

Consensus Preference Hypothesis

A competing view holds that housing preferences do not vary according to personal characteristics. Merton (1957:137) suggests that all Americans "should strive for the same lofty goals since these are open to all." Normatively prescribed housing is one such goal and thus should be preferred by most Americans. The consensus housing preference hypothesis states that there are a number of social factors operating so that the housing norms are equally internalized among all segments of the population. Thus, the vast majority of Americans should prefer single family home ownership regardless of their personal characteristics because it is the only housing situation which satisfies all four housing norms. Other housing situations will be preferred according to the number of housing norms they satisfy, regardless of personal characteristics.

As indicated in Chapter 3, the housing norms of ownership, detached structure, private outside space, and conventionality are widely accepted by Americans. As a result, preferences for housing situations satisfying all or most of the norms are much stronger than preferences for other housing environments. It was inferred at that point that the pattern of housing preferences holds for everybody. Morris and Winter (1978:286) represent this view when they state: "The conclusion is that the norm for ownership of a single-family house is pervasive throughout all classes and ethnic groups in the United States. The overwhelming proportion of the existing evidence supports that conclusion." Similarly, Michelson (1976:125) suggests: "There does not appear to be evidence that rich people and poor people by that criterion alone have significantly different environmental needs." Finally, Lindamood and Hanna (1979:81) propose that all people "aspire to middle-class American normatively defined housing." Thus, single family home ownership is the housing situation which should be preferred overwhelmingly by all Americans, regardless of differences in personal characteristics, according to the consensus housing preference hypothesis.

Some of the social factors operating to minimize differences in housing preferences across Americans have been discussed previously. However, we will now spell these factors out in a more systematic fashion. It can be argued that five separate, although interrelated to some extent, social factors determine the holding of common housing preferences: mass media, observation, economics, prestige, and symbol of self. Because of the existence of these societal influences, people can internalize the housing norms without really experiencing housing situations satisfying these norms. Thus, most Americans should prefer single family home ownership.

Housing norms are transmitted to a considerable extent by the mass media. Ladd (1972:114) suggests that housing images are determined primarily by motion pictures, television, and magazines. In fact, her respondents described houses like "those you see in magazines" (Ladd, 1972:114). Montgomery and Kivlin (1962), Montgomery and McCabe (1973), and Lindamood and Hanna (1979) arrive at the same conclusion. Magazines often have visual layouts of beautiful single family homes. Motion pictures which have plots involving families typically place these families in single family homes. Television shows also portray families living in single family homes (e.g., "Eight is Enough," and "My Three Sons"). Rarely is the multiple family dwelling or mobile home represented in a favorable light by the mass media.

Observation is also important in determining housing preferences. Presently, about two-thirds of American households currently reside in single family homes that they own or are buying (U.S. Bureau of the Census, 1979:1). Thus, most people have been raised in the environment of a single family home or at least have come into extensive contact with it. Even if one does not actually live in a single family home, the homes of friends, relatives, and acquaintances are often of the single family detached dwelling type. Further, the single family home is observed during travel and visitation. Thus, Americans should prefer this housing environment because it is the one most frequently observed (Ladd, 1972; Montgomery and McCabe, 1973).

Economic factors are important in the formation of housing preferences. As suggested earlier, housing is one of the few investments that people make which has traditionally increased in value. This is especially true in times of rapid inflation such as that experienced in recent years. Single family homes which are owned are considered the best financial investment, followed by the other ownership options. Homes which are rented are not considered a good investment. Thus, home ownership satisfies the financial goals of investment. Further, home ownership provides economic security—one can borrow against the home mortgage, obtain cash by selling the home, or keep the home after the mortgage is paid for retirement.

Owning a nice single family home shows that a family is a success in the eyes of the society; it is one way of showing others that a family has done well in the world. Thus, the prestige value of single family home ownership certainly influences housing preferences. Zey-Ferrell, et al. (1977:234) state that "the house and its location are basic in establishing the social status of a person or a family." Rosow (1948:752) similarly stresses the prestige value of the home as an influence for single family home ownership. Since people want their friends to socially approve of their housing, they seek to obtain normatively prescribed housing environments. The housing situation which receives the greatest amount of prestige is the single family home which is owned; therefore, Americans prefer it regardless of their personal characteristics.

Finally, people select housing which reflects a symbol of self. Cooper (1972:32) suggests that people prefer a single family home because of the "need for a house form in which the self and the family unit can be seen as separate, unique, private, and protected." We all tend to view ourselves as distinct individuals, and a detached dwelling reinforces that view. Single family homes also reflect individualism, independence, and stability (Rosow, 1948). Mobile homes and multiple family homes do not reflect a symbol of self since they are perceived as unstable and lacking in privacy.

The five social forces just described result in the leveling of any differences in housing preferences. Thus, the consensus housing preference hypothesis posits that there are no differences in stated housing preferences according to current housing location, current housing situation, household composition, and social class. The competing hypotheses are as follows:

1.   Differential housing preference hypothesis. Housing norms are not equally internalized among all segments of the American population; thus, housing preferences differ according to variations in personal characteristics.

2.   Consensus housing preference hypothesis. There are certain forces operating at the societal level which ensure that the housing norms are

internalized among all segments of the American population; thus, normatively prescribed housing is preferred regardless of personal characteristics.

EVIDENCE FROM PAST RESEARCH

Few studies have empirically examined the relationships between housing preferences and personal characteristics. Although several studies have touched on the topic they have not systematically examined the relationships empirically, and are therefore of little use for comparative purposes. An extensive review of previously published research resulted in the identification of 18 studies which have reported data concerning the relationships between housing preferences and personal characteristics. These 18 studies are identical to those reviewed in the previous two chapters with one exception: Winter and Morris (1976) is included here even though it is based on the same data base as Morris and Winter (1976) which has been previously discussed. The former focuses on the income-housing preference relationship while the latter focuses on the occupation-housing preference relationship. All of the important studies examining the relationships between housing preferences and personal characteristics are listed in Table 8.

Table 8 is a review of literature table summarizing the existing empirical evidence of the relationships between housing preferences and personal characteristics. The personal characteristics employed in the table are those which were measured in the Washington study: rural-urban residence, tenure status, structure type, household size, age, sex, marital status, income, education, and occupation. Thus, it will be possible to compare the relationships found by previous research efforts with those revealed by our own effort in Washington. An "X" in the table indicates that a relationship between a particular personal characteristic and housing preferences was found by a study. An "0" indicates that a possible relationship between a particular personal characteristic and housing preferences was examined by a study, but none was found. If the space linking a study and personal characteristic is blank, the study did not assess whether a relationship exists between that personal characteristic and housing preferences.

The table's purpose is to reveal the existence of bivariate relationships between housing preferences and personal characteristics. Unfortunately, it is not possible to indicate the strength of the bivariate relationships. Many of the studies presented in Table 8 do not report any measures of association,

Table 8. Personal Characteristics Found to be Related to Housing Preferences in Previous Research

Study	Residence	Tenure Status	Structure Type	Household Size	Age	Sex	Marital Status	Income	Education	Occupation
Hinshaw and Allott (1972)			O					O		
Montgomery and McCabe (1973)	X				O			X	X	
Morris and Winter (1976)								O		O
Winter and Morris (1976)[a]								O		
Michelson (1966)	O				O			O	O	O
Michelson (1967)	O				O	O		O	O	O
McCray and Day (1977)	O									
Williams (1971)	X	X	X	O	O			X	X	X
Montgomery and Kivlin (1962)	O	X			O			O		
Caplow (1948)										
Rosow (1948)									X	X
Ladd (1972)			O							
Rushing (1970)								X		
McKown (1975)										
Canter and Thorne (1972)			O							
Beicher (1970)								X	X	
Thornburg (1975)			O							
Gerardi (1976)								X		

NOTE: An X indicates that the relevant study found a significant relationship between a particular personal characteristic and housing preferences. An O means no relationship was found.

[a]Same study as Morris and Winter (1976), but focuses on income instead of occupation.

and it is not possible to compute them based on the information given by these studies. In fact, several of the studies do not even report percentage differences; rather, they merely state that some form of relationship exists or does not exist. This paucity of information is an accurate reflection of the poor state of previous research conducted on the relationships between housing preferences and personal charactersitics.

In addition to the limitation of reporting only whether bivariate relationships between housing preferences and personal characteristics are found in the relevant literature, the results presented in Table 8 suffer from other shortcomings. First, the studies differ in the manner in which they measure housing preferences. A majority of the studies only include a measure of single family home ownership preference. Others tap structure type preferences without considering tenure status preferences, and still others measure tenure status preferences without considering structure type preferences. The single study which examines a wide variety of housing preferences is Williams (1971). Second, the studies differ with regard to their measurement of personal characteristics. They do not measure the relevant personal characteristics in the same manner. Further, none of the studies entails an examination of all the personal characteristics of interest to us. In fact, many of the studies examine the relationships between housing preferences and only one or two personal characteristics. Finally, there is wide variation in the sample frame, sample size, time period in which the data were collected, and the detail employed to describe the data across the 18 studies. Thus, considerable caution must be taken when comparing the results reported by the various studies.

Despite these shortcomings, there are several advantages which accrue to constructing a literature review table. First, the table provides a concise means by which previously unrelated research efforts can be compared. At the same time, the table suggests the inconsistency of the studies. Future research efforts need to be conducted and described in a more scientific manner if a cumulative knowledge base of the relationships between housing preferences and personal characteristics is to be built. The table also reveals that contradictory findings have been reported in the literature. Often previous studies have been content in presenting a vague statement suggesting that there either is or is not some form of relationship between housing preferences and personal characteristics. This table reveals instances in which relationships were found and other instances in which no relationships were discovered. Therefore, vague statements such as "all Americans prefer single family homes" simply cannot be made given the available evidence. The table clarifies the existing evidence and reveals inconsistencies within it.

What does the information presented in Table 8 tell us? The major finding is that there is a great deal of inconsistency in the results of previous research. Neither of the two competing hypotheses receives unequivocal support from the overall findings of previous research efforts. Of the various personal characteristics examined with regard to housing preferences, 16 relationships were discovered. This compares to 23 instances in which a possible relationship between a particular personal characteristic and housing preferences was examined but none was discovered. In several other cases the studies contained in Table 8 failed to assess whether relationships between housing preferences and personal characteristics existed. Indeed, marital status was not examined by any of the studies with regard to housing preferences.

Several of the personal characteristics were found to be related to housing preferences by some studies. No relationships were found between housing preferences and household size, age, and sex. Only tenure status was found to be related to housing preferences by all studies which considered that variable. The personal characteristics of residence, structure type, income, education, and occupation received mixed support in terms of their relationships with housing preferences. The social class variables of income, education, and occupation appear to have been studied to the greatest extent and have been found to be related to housing preferences in several instances. The specific findings displayed in Table 8 will be discussed in the next section of this chapter.

Given the inconsistent results reported in the literature, we will proceed to examine the possible relationships between housing preferences and personal characteristics in some detail. We will conduct this examination by systematically measuring the relationships between housing preferences and the personal characteristics contained in each of the four major demographic categories: current housing location, current housing situation, household composition, and social class. In discussing each potential relationship, we will be concerned with two bodies of evidence. First, the pertinent results presented in the literature review table will be employed to determine the extent to which the literature reveals a relationship. Second, the Washington survey will be examined to determine whether a possible relationship exists.

Following the procedure used in Chapter 3, we will utilize both questionnaire items from the Washington survey to determine the influence of personal characteristics on housing preferences. For the first question, the dependent variables are the combined percentage of respondents selecting a particular housing situation as either their first or second preference. For the second question, the dependent variables are the percentage of respondents stating that they would consider living in a particular housing situation.

HOW PERSONAL CHARACTERISTICS INFLUENCE PREFERENCES

Current Housing Location

As displayed in Table 8, five studies have previously examined the possibility of an extant relationship between current housing location (i.e., rural-urban residence) and housing preferences. Mixed support for the competing hypotheses is found in the literature, as two studies have found a relationship between residence and housing preferences compared to three studies which have not discovered such a relationship. Thus, based on previous empirical research we cannot arrive at a decision with regard to which of the two hypotheses is more tenable.

Michelson (1967) predicted that childhood residence affects housing preferences. Being raised in a rural environment leads to a desire for both detached dwellings and spacious yards. Yet, in his research Michelson found no differences between respondents with differing rural-urban backgrounds and a preference for a single family detached house. Montgomery and Kivlin (1962) found no differences in housing preferences according to current rural-urban residence. Both rural and urban respondents stated a preference for the typical American home--namely, the single family detached dwelling. Finally, McCray and Day (1977) found that the housing preferences of rural and urban residents were similar. Although there were some rural-urban differences in housing quality and satisfaction, both rural and urban respondents "desired a modern brick home with characteristics typical of the middle-class suburban single family house" (McCray and Day, 1977:249).

The two studies which reported the existence of a residence-housing preference relationship do not offer over-powering evidence. Montgomery and McCabe (1973) found that rural residents were more likely to prefer new, single family, well-equipped dwellings than were urban residents. However, both rural and urban respondents stated a strong preference for "suburban modern housing" (Montgomery and McCabe, 1973:10). Williams (1971) found that rural-urban background influenced the strength of preference directed at the townhouse structure type. Whereas 19 percent of those raised in rural areas stated that they would find a townhouse acceptable, 37 percent of those with an urban background found a townhouse acceptable (Williams, 1971:551). However, Williams did not find rural-urban background to be related to any of the other several housing structure types studied.

Two indicators of respondents' rural-urban residence are measured in the Washington study. The first indicator is size of largest city in the respondents' county of residence. This indicator is designed to tap overall population density in the area in which respondents currently reside. In addition, it reflects access to metropolitan services. Respondents living in metropolitan counties (generally counties containing a city of at least 50,000 residents) have greater access to metropolitan services than do respondents living in nonmetropolitan counties. The second indicator of residence is somewhat narrower than the first, as it measures the size of city or town in which respondents live. It is designed to reflect the degree of urbanization of a more restricted geographical area.

Results obtained for the two indicators are similar, as shown in Table 9. When the combined first and second preferences of respondents are examined, it is discovered that preferences for living in a single family dwelling, regardless of whether rented or owned, did not vary to a significant degree according to the level of urbanization of current residence. The largest percentage difference in preference for single family home ownership is only 4 percent for current county size and 6 percent for current city size. Similarly, the percentage differences with regard to the preference of renting a single family home are small. Further, there is not a perfect linear relationship between current housing location and preferences for a single family home. It appears that those respondents living in medium-size counties and cities tended to prefer the single family home options to a slightly greater extent than did other respondents.

Owning a mobile home and lot, reflecting a willingness to sacrifice conventionality, was preferred to a greater degree by rural residents as opposed to urban residents. Whereas only 17.4 percent of those living in cities of at least 500,000 gave this choice as either their first or second preference, 44.9 percent of those living in places of less than 2,500 selected it. A similar result is found with regard to current county size, as a 23.1 percentage difference exists between those respondents living in the most urbanized counties and those living in the least urbanized counties, with the option of owning a mobile home and lot increasing in popularity in a linear fashion from

Table 9.   Selection of Housing Situation as First or Second Preference, by Current Housing Location (Percent)

Current Housing Location Variables[a]	N	First or Second Preference						
		Buy Single Family House	Buy Mobile Home and Lot	Rent Single Family House	Buy Townhouse	Rent Duplex	Rent Apartment	Buy Mobile Home on Rented Space
County Size:								
Largest city under 10,000	(151)	77.5	45.7	17.9	8.6	9.9	7.3	5.3
Largest city of 10,000-49,999	(611)	78.1	40.4	23.9	12.3	11.0	9.7	6.9
Largest city of 50,000-149,999	(534)	81.5	39.3	22.1	17.4	9.9	6.9	7.9
Largest city of 150,000-499,999	(525)	78.3	33.7	22.1	16.0	15.2	10.9	7.6
Largest city of 500,000 or over	(906)	79.0	22.6	22.7	31.1	11.0	12.5	6.5
Gamma		.01	-.25	.01	.35	.03	.13	-.01
Chi Square		2.64	79.65*	2.66	112.35*	9.19	13.24	1.94
City Size:								
Under 2,500	(316)	79.4	44.9	21.8	14.2	6.3	7.3	7.3
2,500-9,999	(301)	80.7	40.5	24.9	12.3	9.3	5.0	7.0
10,000-24,999	(474)	81.4	40.9	23.4	16.2	7.8	7.2	7.8
25,000-49,999	(473)	80.5	35.1	22.2	19.0	13.1	9.1	7.0
50,000-149,999	(167)	80.2	24.0	16.8	32.3	13.8	13.2	6.0
150,000-499,999	(431)	78.2	32.3	21.6	16.5	16.7	12.1	7.0
500,000 or over	(545)	75.4	17.4	24.2	31.0	13.0	16.0	6.6
Gamma		-.07	-.26	.0	.23	.18	.26	-.03
Chi Square		7.51	108.22*	5.57	82.51*	30.70*	40.29*	.90

[a] Gamma is reported if the independent variable can be appropriately treated as ordinal, while Cramer's V is reported if it is nominal.

* Significant at .001 level.

urban to rural counties. Interestingly, no relationship exists between a preference for owning a mobile home on rented space and rural-urban residence. This option is generally disliked by all respondents regardless of residence. Perhaps the absence of land ownership is a major factor why rural residents look unfavorably on this housing alternative.

All three housing options that require giving up a detached structure (i.e., owning a townhouse, renting a duplex, and renting an apartment) were favored to a greater degree by urban residents. Actually, the percentage differences between rural and urban residents are not that substantial for the preferences of renting an apartment (difference of 8.7 percent between largest and smallest city size) and renting a duplex (difference of 6.7 percent between largest and smallest city size). However, the relationship is dramatic for the multiple family dwelling option entailing ownership, as 31.1 percent of those living in counties containing a city of at least 500,000 preferred owning a townhouse, compared to 8.6 percent of those living in counties with a largest city of less than 10,000.

Switching to our second set of data, the extent to which respondents would consider living in a particular housing situation, we find strikingly similar results. The first two rows in Table 10 show the relationships between current county location and the seven housing preferences. Identical to the results presented in Table 9, the correlations between the two residence measures and the preferences of single family home ownership and renting a single family home are not significant. No relationship was found between owning a mobile home on rented space and rural-urban residence as well. The correlations with regard to owning a mobile home and lot and county size ($r = -.1225$) and city size ($r = -.1392$) are significant and positive. Thus, as previously found, rural residents preferred owning a mobile home and lot to a greater extent than did urban residents. Finally, the three multiple family options were preferred to a statistically significant greater extent by urban as opposed to rural residents (r's range from .0590 to .1653).

Although the results produced by the two data sets are essentially the same, Table 10 does clarify the relationships displayed in Table 9. Namely, the relationships that do exist between housing preferences and current housing location are not large ones. The largest correlation found is only .1653 (between owning a townhouse and county size), which we would have to consider weak at best. Similarly, the gammas reported in Table 9 are relatively small, the largest one being .35 (again between owning a townhouse and county size). Thus, even if relationships do exist, it is important to realize that they are relatively weak.

Table 10.   Correlation Matrix of Dependent and Independent Variables

Independent Variables[a]	Housing Preferences (Dependent Variables)						
	Buy Single Family House	Buy Mobile Home and Lot	Rent Single Family House	Rent Duplex	Rent Apartment	Buy Townhouse	Buy Mobile Home on Rented Space
County size	.0102	-.1225*	.0352	.0590*	.0999*	.1653*	-.0146
City size	-.0433	-.1392*	.0175	.0985*	.1345*	.1358*	-.0024
Tenure status	-.0138	.0139	-.1195*	-.1141*	-.0742*	-.0477	-.0163
Structure type:							
Mobile	-.0954*	.2622*	-.0326	-.0552	-.0500	-.0731*	.1390*
Multiple family	-.1452*	-.0408	.1889*	.2629*	.2949*	.1399*	.0501
Single family	.1895*	-.1079*	-.1532*	-.2050*	-.2256*	-.0796*	-.1236*
Household size	.2020*	-.0296	-.0707*	-.2270*	-.3029*	-.0886*	-.1163*
Age	-.3120*	-.0287	-.1797*	.0305	.1917*	-.0847*	.1278*
Sex	-.0293	-.0219	-.0299	-.0715*	-.0623*	.0114	-.0038
Marital status	.1457*	.0182	-.1686*	-.2160*	-.2472*	-.1046*	-.0539
Income	.1687*	-.1420*	-.1523*	-.1437*	-.1349*	.1344*	-.1106*
Education	.1704*	-.1854*	-.0464	.0533	.0052	.2219*	-.1217*
Occupation	.0648*	-.1536*	-.0348	.0591	.0628	.1400*	-.0415

[a]For those cases where the coefficient's direction is unclear the following applies: A positive coefficient means that urban residents prefer a particular housing choice more than rural residents (county size and city size); owners prefer it more than renters (tenure status); those presently living in the structure type indicated prefer it more than those who do not (structure type); men prefer it more than women (sex); those married prefer it more than those who are unmarried (marital status); and white-collar workers prefer it more than blue-collar workers (occupation).

* Significant at .001 level.

Based on the results presented above, we can arrive at some tentative conclusions. First, rural residents found owning a mobile home and lot more acceptable than did urban residents in the Washington study. Second, urban residents were more likely to prefer owning a townhouse than were rural residents. Given the percentage differences and measures of association these two preferences appear to be the only ones related to rural-urban residence. No relationships were found between current housing location and the preferences for the two single family home options and owning a mobile home on rented space, while slight but substantively insignificant relationships were found between rural-urban residence and the options of renting a duplex and renting an apartment.

In terms of the implications of these results on our two competing hypotheses, both receive some support. Preference for single family home ownership, which is the only option satisfying all four housing norms, does not vary according to residence. Thus, both rural and urban residents have internalized the norms resulting in the overwhelming preference for single family home ownership. Four of the remaining six preferences similarly did not vary significantly according to rural-urban residence. These results tend to support the consensus housing preference hypothesis. Only in the case of owning a townhouse, satisfying two and one-half norms, and owning a mobile home and lot, satisfying three norms, did current housing location affect housing preferences. In these two instances the differential housing preference hypothesis receives some support. It appears that rural residents are more likely to give up the norm for conventionality while urban residents are more likely to give up the norm for a detached dwelling and perhaps the norm for private outside space. However, it is important to realize that the number of respondents stating a preference for either of these two options is relatively small, and the differences in support according to residence (as indicated by the measures of association) are relatively small.

Current Housing Situation

The next set of relationships to be examined involves current housing situation and housing preferences. Current housing situation refers to structure type and tenure status. This is a particularly important set of relationships to examine because quite different implications result if people are presently living in their preferred housing situation (regardless of what it is) than if they have not yet satisfied their preference. The first possibility suggests that people have been successful in realizing their preferred housing environment, or perhaps have adapted preferences to current housing situation, while the other possibility suggests that despite the experience of living in a certain housing situation it remains undesirable.

Only two previous studies have examined the relationships between tenure status and housing preferences. Both studies found evidence of a relationship--namely, owners preferred housing situations involving ownership while renters were more likely to prefer renting a home. However, the differences in housing preferences according to current tenure status found in these studies were not substantial. Williams (1971:551) found that renters were slightly more likely to prefer a townhouse (we can only infer that the townhouse choice entailed renting) than were owners. Tenure status was not related to any of the other housing options studied. Caplow (1948) found slight differences in tenure status preferences depending on current tenure status. Whereas 73.4 percent of renters preferred to own a home, 86.7 percent of owners preferred to own a home (Caplow, 1948:726). Thus, even though there does appear to be a relationship between housing preferences and tenure status, both current owners and renters preferred home ownership.

Of the five studies assessing the relationships between housing structure type and housing preferences, only one found any type of relationship. Williams (1971:551) found that apartment dwellers were more likely to prefer a townhouse than were single family home dwellers. Current structure type was not related to any other housing preferences in that study. Hinshaw and Allott (1972) hypothesized that it is difficult for most people to perceive environments foreign to their personal experiences; therefore, people prefer the kinds of environments with which they are familiar. However, their research revealed that respondents preferred single family home ownership regardless of current structure type (Hinshaw and Allott, 1972:104-105). Ladd's (1972:111-112) study of low-income blacks living in apartments revealed that these people preferred single family dwellings, not apartments. Canter and Thorne (1972:25) found similar results: people did not necessarily prefer the type of housing to which they were accustomed. Finally, Thornburg (1975:196) also found that current structure type did not affect housing preferences. Her respondents residing in multiple family dwellings overwhelmingly preferred single family homes.

In the Washington study respondents were asked questions concerning both their current tenure status and their current housing structure type. Table 11 shows the relationships between housing preferences and respondents' current housing situation for our first set of data. The overall relationship between tenure status and housing preferences is rather

Table 11. Selection of Housing Situation as First or Second Preference, by Current Housing Situation (Percent)

Current Housing Situation Variables[a]	N	First or Second Preference						
		Buy Single Family House	Buy Mobile Home and Lot	Rent Single Family House	Buy Townhouse	Rent Duplex	Rent Apartment	Buy Mobile Home on Rented Space
Tenure Status:								
Rent	(582)	69.8	20.1	39.9	16.8	18.7	17.7	4.8
Own	(2046)	80.6	35.8	17.4	20.9	9.9	8.4	7.7
Gamma		.29	.38	-.52	.13	-.35	-.40	.24
Chi Square		30.90*	50.47*	129.62*	4.36	32.75*	41.33*	5.24
Housing Structure Type:								
Apt. building	(247)	53.8	11.3	27.9	21.5	25.5	34.0	6.1
Townhouse	(37)	62.2	13.5	37.8	35.1	10.8	16.2	2.7
Duplex	(90)	83.3	25.6	36.7	13.3	21.1	8.9	2.2
Mobile home	(170)	61.2	72.9	5.9	4.1	10.0	4.1	21.2
Apt. in a house	(45)	62.2	22.2	26.7	20.0	20.0	13.3	11.1
Single family house	(2149)	83.1	33.3	21.9	20.8	9.5	7.7	6.2
Cramer's V		.24	.26	.13	.11	.16	.25	.15
Chi Square		159.58*	185.98*	47.70*	35.93*	67.66*	177.47*	60.25*

[a]Gamma is reported if the independent variable can be appropriately treated as ordinal, while Cramer's V is reported if it is nominal.

* Significant at .001 level.

straightforward. Respondents owning their home preferred the options entailing ownership, while those renting their home tended to select one of the rent options to a greater extent. Only in the instances of owning a townhouse and owning a mobile home on rented space was no statistically significant relationship found. This finding indicates that there is a group of respondents who prefer to rent rather than own a home. It also appears that another group of respondents exists which has achieved ownership but is willing to give it up.

The above results generally support those findings reported in the previous literature, and offer support to the differential housing preference hypothesis. However, our data reveal the same type of relationship as the Caplow study: namely, those currently renting their home still preferred ownership. As shown in Table 11, even those currently renting their home preferred single family home ownership (69.8 percent) over the three rent options (support for these ranged from 17.7 to 39.9 percent), although the differences are smaller when contrasted with those owning their home (80.6 percent selected single family home ownership as their first or second preference, compared to between 7.7 and 17.4 percent who selected one of the rent options). Thus, the norm for home ownership is a strong one regardless of current tenure status, and this lends support to the consensus housing preference hypothesis.

Table 11 contains several important findings with regard to current housing structure type and preferences. Of utmost significance, single family home ownership was more often selected as the first or second preference by residents of all alternative structure types than was a preference for living in their present type of residence. This suggests that experience in an alternative structure type does not significantly reduce people's desire to live in housing which meets the norm for a detached structure. The only exception to this pattern is mobile home dwellers, who preferred owning a mobile home and lot (72.9 percent) over single family home ownership (61.2 percent). In contrast, between 21.1 and 35.1 percent of those living in multiple family dwellings gave their current structure type as their first or second preference, while between 53.8 and 83.3 percent stated a preference for single family home ownership. Current occupants of a duplex ranked that structure type as only their fourth preference (21.1 percent), allocating it less support than owning a mobile home and lot (25.6 percent), renting a single family home (36.7 percent), as well as owning a single family home (83.3 percent). Those residing in a single family home, by far the largest number of respondents, preferred housing situations in accordance to the extent to which each satisfied the four housing norms. Those housing situations meeting few of the norms were preferred by only a small proportion of those respondents currently living in a single family home.

Turning back to Table 10, it is possible to consider the second set of data with regard to current housing situation and housing preferences. The third row presents the correlations found between tenure status and the seven housing preferences. Three of these correlations are statistically significant, all involving the three rent options. It appears that renters were slightly more likely to prefer renting a home than were owners. However, the correlations are all weak for these three preferences (r's range from -.0742 to -.1195). The correlation coefficients are almost nonexistent for the other four housing preferences.

When attention is shifted to the next three rows in Table 10, we can examine the relationships between structure type and housing preferences. For this part of the analysis, dummy variables were created for the three basic structure types: mobile home, multiple family home, and single family home. The results obtained are precisely what might be expected if we predicted that structure type influenced housing preferences. Those living in mobile homes were more likely to prefer owning a mobile home and lot (r = .2622) and owning a mobile home on rented space (r = .1390); it is negatively associated with the remaining housing preferences. Those living in multiple family homes were more likely to prefer one of the multiple family home options (r's range from .1399 to .2949). Finally, those currently residing in a single family home were more likely to prefer single family home ownership (r = .1895). This last structure type was negatively associated with the other housing preferences. However, the correlations found are weak (the largest being .2949). Even though there does appear to be a tendency for those living in a particular housing structure type to prefer that situation more than other respondents, a majority of respondents in every structure type still preferred single family home ownership. This probably accounts for the low correlation coefficients.

The review of literature and consideration of our own data results in mixed support for the two hypotheses. Current housing situation is somewhat related to housing preferences. Owners were more likely to prefer housing situations entailing ownership than were renters, and vice versa. Respondents living in a particular structure type were more likely to prefer a housing situation entailing that structure type. However, as clearly displayed in Table 11, a majority of both owners and renters preferred single family home ownership. Further, a majority of respondents in all structure types (with one exception) preferred single family home ownership. Thus, most respondents have indeed internalized the housing norms of ownership, detached structure, private outside space, and conventionality.

Household Composition

As suggested earlier, there are some good reasons for expecting household composition to be associated with housing preferences. However, the literature does not support such an expectation. Only seven studies have examined the possibility of relationships between housing preferences and the four household composition variables, and none have found any relationships. In fact, marital status has never been studied in relation to housing preferences. Both Michelson (1967) and Williams (1971) found that sex was not related to housing preferences. Even though women appear to be more greatly affected by their residential surrounding than are men, this does not seem to lead to the development of differential housing preferences. Williams (1971) similarly found that household size was not related to housing preferences. The household composition variable which has received the most consideration is age of the head of household. Studies conducted by Michelson (1966), Montgomery and McCabe (1973), and Williams (1971) produced results indicating that age of household head made no difference with regard to housing preferences. Even the detailed analysis conducted by Michelson (1967) found that age did not influence preference for a single family home.

It should be pointed out that other variables could be included in our discussion on household composition and housing preferences. Specifically, race might be predicted to influence housing preferences. Belcher (1970), Hanna and Lindamood (1979), and Hinshaw and Allott (1972), have studied the possibility of such a relationship and have all come to the same conclusion: race does not significantly affect housing preferences. The reason race is not included in our analysis is that it was not measured by the Washington survey. Another variable which might be included is family life cycle. Studies conducted by Michelson (1977) and Montgomery and McCabe (1973) have considered family life cycle and found it to be unrelated to housing preferences. Rather than form a family life cycle variable, we have decided to analyze its various components (i.e., household size, age of head of household, and marital status) separately in order to reveal as much information as possible about the household composition-housing preferences relationships.

The relationships between housing preferences and the four household composition variables for the first set of data are presented in Table 12. It was expected that household size, the first measure of household composition, would be related to housing preferences--namely, the larger the household, the greater the need for a housing situation likely to provide considerable space. This expectation is generally supported by the data, as preference for single family home ownership increased as household size increased--going from a low of 57.3 percent of those in one-person households preferring this choice to a high of around 90 percent of those in households of four persons or more supporting it. However, there appears to be no significant relationship when renting a single family home is the variable under consideration, suggesting that size is not the only reason why larger households prefer certain housing situations. The mobile home options provided ambiguous results--smaller households were more likely to prefer owning a mobile home on rented space while larger households (up to a certain size) were slightly more apt to prefer owning a mobile home and lot. The smallest households were much more likely than the largest households to state a preference for renting a duplex (24.6 versus 6.6 percent) and renting an apartment (22.6 versus 3.3 percent). Owning a townhouse was slightly more preferred as household size increased. These findings suggest that not only is a detached structure important to large households, perhaps because of the outside space and the larger size it may imply, but ownership is also strongly desired.

The results obtained from our second set of data, seventh row in Table 10, support those findings discussed above. Six of the seven possible relationships between household size and housing preferences are significant. The three more notable correlations are between household size and single family home ownership (r = .2020), renting a duplex (r = -.2270) and renting an apartment (r = -.3029). As household size increased, preference for single family home ownership increased while preference for multiple family dwellings involving renting decreased. Again, however, the correlations are rather weak. Further, it is important to realize that a majority of respondents, regardless of household size, selected single family home ownership as either their first or second preference (Table 12).

The remainder of Table 12 deals with characteristics of the respondents who answered the questionnaire for their household. Age appears to be the most important of the household composition variables when examining housing preferences. Not only is the age variable significantly related to each of the seven housing preferences, but the gammas obtained are moderate (gammas range from -.06 to -.59). Preference for single family home ownership declined dramatically as age increased (dropping from a high of 93.6 percent of those between 25 and 34 selecting this choice as their first or second preference to a low of 45.0 percent of those 65 or over). Thus, it appears that the need to conform to all four housing norms declines somewhat with age. On the other hand, respondents in the younger age groups showed a strong desire to conform to the four housing norms by overwhelmingly preferring single family home ownership, suggesting that these norms are still powerful motivators of people's housing preferences. The same general pattern, although not to as noticeable a degree, occurs when we assess the relationship between age and preferences for renting a single family home and owning a townhouse. Respondents in the older age categories were more apt to express a preference for renting a duplex, renting an apartment, and owning a mobile home on rented space. These findings suggest that the norms for ownership and outside space are probably not as important to older people; rather, many in this age group desire to rent a home in a multiunit structure.

The second set of data reveals the same basic results with reference to age and housing preferences, shown in the eighth column of Table 10. The correlation for age and single family home ownership ($r = -.3120$) is the largest reported in the entire table. Thus, it is clear that age influences preference for single family home ownership. The largest positive correlations found are for renting an apartment ($r = .1917$) and owning a mobile home on rented space ($r = .1278$). The elderly were more likely to opt for these two choices than were those respondents in the younger age groups.

Sex does not seem to be an important variable in the examination of housing preferences. As shown in Table 12, only two of the relationships reach statistical significance and even here the gammas are not large (gamma = -.27 for renting a duplex; gamma = -.21 for renting an apartment). In fact, the largest percentage difference between males and females with regard to housing preferences is only 5.5 percent. Both males and females overwhelmingly preferred single family home ownership (80.9 and 76.7 percent respectively). Table 10 shows the same general lack of association between sex and housing preferences. The correlations range from -.0038 (owning a mobile home on rented space) to a high of -.0715 (renting a duplex). Despite the low correlations, the same two preferences found to be statistically significant in Table 12 are also statistically significant here. However, it seems apparent that sex does not influence housing preferences to a substantively significant extent.

Table 12. Selection of Housing Situation as First or Second Preference, by Household Composition (Percent)

		First or Second Preference						
Household Composition Variables[a]	N	Buy Single Family House	Buy Mobile Home and Lot	Rent Single Family House	Buy Townhouse	Rent Duplex	Rent Apartment	Buy Mobile Home on Rented Space
Household Size:								
One person	(517)	57.3	20.5	22.1	16.6	24.6	22.6	9.1
Two people	(980)	73.6	33.4	19.7	18.3	12.6	11.8	9.8
Three people	(464)	86.4	36.6	24.6	20.3	7.8	4.7	5.8
Four people	(479)	92.7	40.7	22.1	22.8	4.4	3.3	2.7
Five people	(240)	92.5	37.1	25.8	24.2	4.2	3.8	4.2
Six people or over	(121)	89.3	29.8	28.1	22.3	6.6	3.3	2.5
Gamma		.52	.17	.06	.11	- .46	- .52	- .30
Chi Square		260.76*	54.66*	9.34	10.79	132.45*	147.73*	36.52*
Age:								
Under 25	(249)	90.4	39.0	39.8	11.6	8.8	5.6	1.2
25-34	(655)	93.6	31.1	29.0	25.5	7.9	2.4	2.3
35-44	(472)	90.9	35.4	21.8	26.5	5.5	5.3	4.2
45-54	(450)	79.1	38.0	14.9	24.4	10.9	10.0	6.9
55-64	(451)	68.5	36.4	14.4	18.0	14.4	13.5	14.9
65 or over	(362)	45.0	22.4	16.9	5.5	24.3	29.0	13.5
Gamma		- .59	- .06	- .29	- .15	.31	.54	.50
Chi Square		430.96*	31.57*	97.92*	89.19*	89.20*	208.49*	107.07*

Table 12. Continued.

Household Composition Variables[a]	N	First or Second Preference						
		Buy Single Family House	Buy Mobile Home and Lot	Rent Single Family House	Buy Townhouse	Rent Duplex	Rent Apartment	Buy Mobile Home on Rented Space
Sex:								
Female	(1204)	76.7	32.1	22.8	18.1	14.5	12.3	7.6
Male	(1504)	80.9	34.0	22.0	21.7	9.0	8.4	6.6
Gamma		.13	.04	- .02	.11	- .27	- .21	- .07
Chi Square		7.05	.93	.22	5.09	19.84*	10.84*	.83
Marital Status:								
Single	(262)	80.2	19.5	36.6	22.9	18.3	12.6	2.3
Married	(2011)	83.0	36.7	20.6	21.2	8.2	6.9	6.7
Separated or divorced	(239)	75.3	28.9	27.2	16.7	17.6	14.6	7.1
Widowed	(237)	44.3	23.2	17.3	9.3	27.4	31.2	14.3
Cramer's V		.26*	.13	.12	.09	.19*	.23*	.10
Chi Square		192.23*	46.35*	41.07*	21.79*	100.98*	144.62*	29.12*

[a] Gamma is reported if the independent variable can be appropriately treated as ordinal, while Cramer's V is reported if it is nominal.

* Significant at .001 level.

[handwritten marginalia: marital status = great influence]

Finally, marital status is studied in reference to housing preferences. Table 12 reveals that marital status is significantly related to all seven housing preferences. The most interesting finding is that married respondents preferred owning a single family home and owning a mobile home and lot to a greater extent than other marital status groups. Conversely, single households were more apt to prefer renting a single family home and owning a townhouse. The widowed group is an interesting one, as these respondents tended to prefer the multiple family dwellings of renting a duplex and renting an apartment. Not even a majority of the widowed group selected owning a single family home as either their first or second preference (44.3 percent selected this choice).

Marital status was dichotomized (nonmarried versus married) for analysis of the second set of data, but results are similar to those found in Table 12. In Table 10, row 10, it is shown that a statistically significant positive correlation exists between marital status and single family home ownership ($r = .1457$), meaning that married respondents were more likely to prefer this choice than were nonmarried respondents, and statistically significant negative correlations exist between marital status and renting a single family home ($r = -.1686$), renting a duplex ($r = -.2160$), renting an apartment ($r = -.2472$), and owning a townhouse ($r = -.1046$). Thus, those respondents not married tended to prefer housing situations involving multiple family dwellings and/or renting. However, the correlations presented in Table 10 are not large ones, and the gammas presented in Table 12 are relatively small. Thus, marital status does not seem to have a major influence on housing preferences. Further, it is probable that some of this variation in housing preferences according to marital status can be explained by age.

Based on the literature review of household composition and housing preferences, no support was offered that the two groups of variables are related to one another. Interestingly, the data from the Washington study reveal that household composition appears to influence housing preferences to a greater extent than does either current housing location or current housing situation. With regard to some specific relationships, support is given to the differential housing preference hypothesis. This is particularly true in the case of the relationship between age and marital status, and preference for single family home ownership. Here for the first time we find a minority of respondents (those 65 or over and those who are widowed) that selected this option as their first or second preference. However, the consensus housing preference hypothesis also receives some support. Sex is not related to housing preferences, and many of the specific relationships between the household composition variables of household size, age, and marital status, and housing preferences are not significant.

Social Class

We might expect that the higher the respondents' social class, the more likely they were to have internalized the housing norms. Thus, as social class increases preferences for housing situations satisfying the norms should increase. Several studies have been conducted which have considered this predicted association between social class and housing preferences, as shown in the literature review table. In fact, social class has received more attention in the past than the other personal characteristics.

Three measures of social class have been employed in previous research efforts--income, education, and occupation. Half of the studies reported in Table 8 have examined the relationships between income and housing preferences. Of these nine studies, five have found significant relationships. Montgomery and McCabe (1973:10) found that the higher the income the greater the probability of holding a suburban modern housing image. Rushing (1970:377) found that the goal for owning a home was not as salient for low-income people as it was for middle- and high-income people. Williams (1971:550) concluded from his research that "there appears to be a tendency for lower income families to be less likely to find the multi-family types acceptable." Gerardi (1976:4) found that income was slightly related to the preferences for single family home ownership, owning a duplex, owning a townhouse, and owning an apartment (i.e., condominium). Finally, Belcher (1970) suggests that housing is more important to high-income people.

On the other side of the research conducted on the relationships between income and housing preferences are those studies finding no relationships. Studies by Hinshaw and Allott (1972) and Michelson (1966) revealed that income did not influence housing preferences. Montgomery and Kivlin (1962:489) concluded that "by and large the housing wants and expectations of women from families having a lower socioeconomic status were similar to those from families having a higher socioeconomic status." Winter and Morris (1976) have conducted the most rigid test of the possibility of a relationship existing between income and housing preferences, and found no such relationship. Winter and Morris (1976:16) concluded that "neither the literature nor the present set of data provide any support for the proposition that the low income class has different home ownership and structure type norms or aspirations from other income groups."

A total of six studies have considered education and its effect on housing preferences. Montgomery and McCabe (1973:10) found that the higher the education the greater the probability of holding a suburban modern housing image. Rosow (1948) found that education affected ownership preferences. Williams (1971) revealed that higher educational levels increased the probability of preferences for an apartment and a townhouse. Finally, Belcher (1970) found that housing was more important to those with high education and led to increased wants in terms of housing. The two studies conducted by Michelson (1966; 1967) found no relationships between education and housing preferences.

Occupation has received the attention of five studies, two of them showing that it is related to housing preferences. Rosow (1948) found that professional workers preferred ownership to a lower extent than did businessmen. Williams (1971) found that increased occupational prestige led to increased preference for a townhouse. On the other hand, Michelson (1966; 1967) found no relationships between occupation and preference for single family homes. Morris and Winter (1976) also found no relationships. They found only a 0.2 percent difference between blue-collar and white-collar workers in ownership preference, and a 1.1 percent difference in single family home preference (Morris and Winter, 1976:8).

As was the case with the literature reviews of the other personal characteristics, past research provides mixed support for the two competing hypotheses. However, both income and education receive considerable support with regard to their influence on housing preferences, while occupation receives somewhat less support. Table 13 displays the relationships between housing preferences and the three measures of social class utilized in the Washington study. Generally, considerable evidence is given in the table supporting the existence of relationships between social class and housing preferences.

Preference for single family home ownership increased as income, education, and occupational prestige increased. Income is a particularly interesting variable in this context, as 51.2 percent of those households earning under $5,000 stated a preference for single family home ownership, compared to 88.2 percent of those earning $50,000 or over. Middle-income respondents also strongly preferred this choice. A difference of 23.7 percent exists between those respondents with under a high-school education and those who are college graduates, and a difference of 5.5 percent exists between blue-collar workers and white-collar workers. Thus, the single family home ownership preference is strongly influenced by income and education, and not influenced noticeably by occupation.

Owning a mobile home and lot was preferred to a greater extent by those ranking low in social class. This is particularly true in the case of education (42.0 percent of those with less than high-school education selected this housing situation as their first or second preference compared to only 19.9 percent of those with a college education) and occupation (this situation was preferred by 41.8 percent of blue-collar workers compared to 28.1 percent of white-collar workers). A 15.1 percent difference exists between the extreme income categories, with the lower-income group preferring this choice more than the higher-income group. Thus, it appears that respondents in the lower social class grouping may be willing to give up conventionality in order to achieve the norms for a detached structure, ownership, and, to some degree, outside space.

Renting a single family home did not vary significantly according to social class. Owning a mobile home on rented space did vary according to income and education, but no real differences emerged according to occupation (4.0 percent difference between blue-collar and white-collar workers). The multiple family dwelling options including renting were preferred by those of lower social class, particularly when income is considered. Renting a duplex and renting an apartment were preferred by 23.4 and 21.3 percent, respectively, of those households earning under $5,000, compared to 3.9 and 11.8 percent, respectively, of those households earning $50,000 or over. Actually, the differences in preferences for those two choices are small when considering education and occupation. Finally, the other option involving ownership (owning a townhouse) was preferred by those in the higher social class categories, particularly when income is examined (4.9 percent of those earning less than $5,000 preferred it compared to 46.1 percent of those earning $50,000 or over).

Turning to our second set of data, displayed in Table 10, similar results are found. However, a better indication of the significance of the relationships is provided. Income appears to have the strongest influence on housing preferences, as all seven relationships are statistically significant. The correlations vary in strength from a low of -.1106 (owning a mobile home on rented space) to a high of .1687 (owning a single family home). Education produces statistically significant relationships in four instances. The correlations for education are slightly lower than found for income, ranging from .0052 (renting an apartment) to .2219 (owning a townhouse). Occupation produces three statistically significant relationships, with the correlations ranging from -.0348 (renting a single family home) to -.1536 (owning a mobile home and lot). The direction of the various social class correlations generally follows that found in Table 13.

Table 13. Selection of Housing Situation as First or Second Preference, by Social Class (Percent)

First or Second Preference

Social Class Variables[a]	N	Buy Single Family House	Buy Mobile Home and Lot	Rent Single Family House	Buy Townhouse	Rent Duplex	Rent Apartment	Buy Mobile Home on Rented Space
Income:								
Under $5,000	(244)	51.2	28.3	26.2	4.9	23.4	21.3	14.8
$5,000–$9,999	(413)	66.3	32.9	27.1	9.2	18.6	13.6	8.0
$10,000–$14,999	(532)	79.3	37.0	24.8	15.0	11.8	10.5	8.6
$15,000–$19,999	(503)	85.5	41.9	22.3	17.3	9.3	6.2	7.0
$20,000–$24,999	(397)	87.9	34.5	19.9	25.4	7.8	5.3	5.0
$25,000–$34,999	(332)	87.0	29.2	19.6	34.0	6.9	8.4	4.8
$35,000–$49,999	(149)	87.2	16.8	18.8	47.0	6.0	8.7	1.3
$50,000 or over	(76)	88.2	13.2	10.5	46.1	3.9	11.8	2.6
Gamma		.40	-.07	-.13	.45	-.33	-.24	-.28
Chi Square		206.78*	57.98*	19.08	221.30*	76.19*	59.85*	38.65*
Education:								
Under high school	(367)	62.4	42.0	20.2	5.2	13.9	11.4	10.9
High school graduate	(720)	73.9	41.5	20.3	12.4	11.7	11.8	12.1
Some college	(827)	83.0	35.1	22.7	21.4	10.4	9.2	5.7
College graduate	(815)	86.1	19.9	25.2	32.0	11.8	9.3	2.2
Gamma		.33	-.29	.09	.45	-.04	-.08	-.43
Chi Square		104.08*	101.80*	6.51	151.28*	3.07	4.24	67.77*

Table 13. Continued.

		First or Second Preference						
Social Class Variables[a]	N	Buy Single Family House	Buy Mobile Home and Lot	Rent Single Family House	Buy Townhouse	Rent Duplex	Rent Apartment	Buy Mobile Home on Rented Space
Occupation[b]:								
Blue-collar	(1074)	79.1	41.8	24.4	12.2	10.6	7.3	8.7
White-collar	(1289)	84.6	28.1	20.4	29.9	9.9	9.7	4.7
Other	(107)	67.3	19.6	30.8	10.3	28.0	20.6	7.5
Cramer's V		.10	.15	.06	.22	.12	.09	.08
Chi Square		26.71*	59.28*	9.69	118.00*	33.36*	21.91*	14.89*

[a] Gamma is reported if the independent variable can be appropriately treated as ordinal, while Cramer's V is reported if it is nominal.

[b] Blue-collar occupations are private household workers, service workers, farm laborers, farmers, farm managers, laborers (except farm), transportation operators, equipment operators, operators (except transportation or equipment), craftsmen, and clerical workers. White-collar occupations are sales workers, managers, administrators, and professional workers. Other occupations are housewives and students.

* Significant at .001 level.

The data from the Washington study provide mixed support for the two competing hypotheses. Income seems to be the most influential social class variable, as predicted by some of the housing preference literature. Education is somewhat less influential, and occupation appears to exert little influence on housing preferences. A majority of respondents in all three social class categories preferred single family home ownership. Further, several of the specific relationships are not significant, particularly in the case of occupation. However, several of the specific relationships are both statistically and substantively significant. Thus, mixed support is given to the hypotheses. It does seem clear, however, that at least some of the variation in housing preferences is due to the differential internalization of norms. Further, the findings seem congruent with people's actual financial status. Thus, the notion of financial constraints inherent in belonging to a lower social class group may account for some of these differences in housing preferences.

RECAPITULATION AND DISCUSSION

The general question addressed by this chapter is: What effects do personal characteristics have on housing preferences? There exist two competing views regarding an answer to this question. The first view holds that the housing norms are not equally internalized among all segments of the American population. As a result, housing preferences differ depending on the personal characteristics of the people under consideration. We labeled this the differential housing preference hypothesis. The second view holds that because of mass media, observation, economics, prestige, and symbol of self, the housing norms are internalized among all segments of the American population. Thus, normatively prescribed housing is preferred regardless of personal characteristics. We labeled this the consensus housing preference hypothesis.

Which of the two views is correct? Both views receive some support when applied to housing preference studies reported in the literature. Some studies report differences in housing preferences according to personal characteristics, while other studies report no significant differences. However, the consensus housing preference hypothesis does receive slightly more support in the literature, as a majority of studies report an almost universal preference for single family home ownership.

When attention is focused on the Washington survey data mixed results again emerge. At the bivariate level, there are several significant relationships between personal characteristics and housing preferences. It appears that current structure type, household size, age, income, and education are the personal characteristics having the greatest influence on housing preferences. This gives support for the differential housing preference hypothesis. However, the measures of association reported for the relationships between these personal characteristics and housing preferences are not large. Further, many of these personal characteristics are not related to all of the seven housing preferences. Other variables are found to not be related to housing preferences to any considerable extent--namely, current county size, current community size, current tenure status, sex, marital status, and occupation. Given the lack of substantial relationships between these personal characteristics and housing preferences, considerable support is given for the consensus housing preference hypothesis.

At a more general level, it appears that the consensus housing preference hypothesis can be discounted. Although it receives considerable support from previous research as well as the Washington survey data, it does not receive unequivocal support. The hypothesis states that all Americans, regardless of personal characteristics, have the same housing preferences, and this is not the case. The fact that the differential housing preference hypothesis receives any support at all means that the basic premise of the consensus housing preference hypothesis is incorrect.

From a research standpoint, the results presented in this chapter suggest that personal characteristics must be carefully considered in future housing preference research. It does appear that at least some of the 11 personal characteristics influence housing preferences. Knowledge of the housing preferences-personal characteristics relationships is crucial for those in policy decision-making positions as well. In designing and implementing housing programs, it is necessary to gain an understanding of the target population and the housing preferences which it holds. Such knowledge may mean the difference between a housing program's success or failure in the eyes of the people it is designed to help.

Do people have different housing preferences? The answer is "yes," albeit a soft-spoken "yes." Given this conclusion, the question arises as to which of the personal characteristics have the greatest impact on housing preferences. Such a question cannot be accurately answered by an examination of the bivariate relationships presented in this chapter. It can only be answered by conducting a multivariate analysis of the relationship between housing preferences and personal characteristics. This is the task of the next chapter.

5

A Closer Look at the Influence of Personal Characteristics on Housing Preferences

What personal characteristics have the greatest influence on housing preferences? This is an important question to answer. It is possible that some personal characteristics have no influence on housing preferences and, as a result, can be allocated low priority in housing preference research. Other personal characteristics may have a major influence on housing preferences; therefore, they need to be seriously considered when researching housing preferences. We may also discover that different personal characteristics are important to consider depending on the specific housing choice being studied.

To arrive at a better understanding of how personal characteristics influence housing preferences we need to determine the separate and combined contributions of the personal characteristics to variation in the seven housing preferences. The previous analysis of the bivariate relationships between personal characteristics and housing preferences indicates that there is a complex overall relationship between the two sets of variables. This complexity cannot be fully understood by examining the bivariate correlations because they simply indicate the relationship between the independent and dependent variables separately. Further, the bivariate correlations are not sufficient because the various personal characteristics do not represent completely unique determinants. Rather, the personal characteristics are inter-correlated (e.g., county size and city size). As a result, it is difficult to determine from a bivariate analysis the "true" importance of the various personal characteristics. We therefore need to employ a multivariate analysis, so that potentially confounding effects of the personal characteristics on housing preferences can be controlled.

The multivariate statistical technique we will use is multiple regression analysis, a technique which will allow us to determine both the relative and cumulative effects of the various personal characteristics on housing preferences. With regard to the relative effects, the application of simultaneous controls allows us to determine which of the personal characteristics emerge as the most important predictors of housing preferences. The relative importance of each personal characteristic is measured by the size of the standardized regression coefficient. In this manner we can evaluate the relative importance of the personal characteristics in explaining housing preferences.

The determination of relative effects is important for two reasons. First, measurement of the independent effects that each personal characteristic has on housing preferences indicates which of these characteristics have the greatest influence on housing preferences. Those having little or no effect might be excluded from future analyses of housing preferences, while those having strong independent effects should be included in housing preference research. Second, measuring the effect that each of the personal characteristics have on each of the seven housing preferences will suggest which personal characteristics need to be considered for each housing choice. Thus, we can specify the exact personal characteristics that need to be utilized to explain people's preference for a particular housing situation.

With regard to the cumulative effects, multiple regression analysis allows us to determine if the various personal characteristics have a significant impact on housing preferences when considered in combination. Although the bivariate correlations are rather small, it is possible that the multiple correlation coefficients obtained by using all the personal characteristics in a single multivariate model is fairly substantial. This would suggest that several of the personal characteristics need to be considered when explaining housing preferences. On the other hand, we may discover that the various personal characteristics add very little to one another in terms of explaining housing preferences. This would suggest that the use of a large number of personal characteristics to predict housing preferences would not be parsimonious. Thus, future research would incorporate only those few personal characteristics which have the strongest relative effects on housing preferences.

The determination of cumulative effects is particularly important because it provides further evidence regarding the usefulness of the differential housing preference hypothesis. If we find that the multiple coefficients of determination are large, then strong support would be given to the differential housing preference hypothesis. This would indicate that knowledge of personal characteristics leads to a fuller understanding of people's stated housing preferences. On the other hand, if the cumulative effects of the personal characteristics on housing preferences are small, then the utility of the differential housing preference hypothesis would be questioned.

Unfortunately there exists no previous research which has employed a multivariate analysis of housing preferences. Therefore, there is no reason for expecting particular kinds of coefficients to emerge in our analysis. Given the low bivariate relationships found between personal characteristics and housing preferences in past research, however, it is probable that these studies would have been able to account for relatively little of the variation in housing preferences by focusing on the combined effects of several personal characteristics.

MULTIVARIABLE ANALYSIS

Table 14 shows the standardized regression coefficients which result from regressing the housing preferences on all 11 personal characteristics separately. The multiple correlation coefficients and coefficients of determination for each regression are also shown in this table. The standardized regression coefficients are used in Table 14 because they are the best indicators of the relative importance of each independent variable (Kerlinger and Pedhazur, 1973). They can be interpreted as the effects of each independent variable on a particular housing preference, when the effects of all ten of the other independent variables in the regression are controlled. Thus, by examining the size of the coefficients we can observe whether the same personal characteristics which were significantly correlated with housing preferences at the bivariate level are strong predictors of preferences when controlling for the other personal characteristics.

Only the second group of dependent variables obtained in the Washington study is subjected to multivariate analysis: the extent to which respondents considered living in the various housing situations. These dependent variables are used because they can be effectively treated as interval level data. As explained earlier, the extent to which respondents considered living in each of the seven housing situations were coded based on a scale ranging from one to five. The personal characteristics can also be treated as interval level data, as explained in the previous chapter. Given the similarity of results obtained from using the two different groups of dependent variables in the bivariate analysis, there is some justification for using only the second group of dependent variables for the multivariate analysis. However, we are losing some information because the first group of dependent variables included both first and second preferences.

Table 14. Standardized Regression Coefficients, Multiple Correlation Coefficients, and Multiple Coefficients of Determination for the Regression of the Housing Preferences on the Independent Variables

Independent Variables[a]	Housing Preferences (Dependent Variables)						
	Buy Single Family House	Buy Mobile Home and Lot	Rent Single Family House	Rent Duplex	Rent Apartment	Buy Townhouse	Buy Mobile Home on Rented Space
County size	.0371	-.0275	.0108	-.0182	.0152	.0974*	-.0193
City size	-.0467	-.0967*	-.0240	.0396	.0355	.0165	-.0032
Tenure status	-.0424*	-.0116	-.0658*	-.0583*	-.0266	-.0186	-.0178
Structure type:							
Mobile	-.0476	.2580*	-.1141*	-.1206*	-.0558	-.0456	.1097*
Multiple family	-.0672	.0670	-.0215	.0670	.1692*	.0590	.0818
Single family	.1101*	.0463	-.1702*	-.1633*	-.0711	-.0606	-.0032
Household size	.0055	-.0326	.0230	-.0964*	-.1377*	-.1050*	-.0524*
Age	-.2918*	.0101	-.1444*	-.0438*	.1857*	-.0300	.1084*
Sex	.0321	.0166	.0112	.0509*	-.0394	-.0054	.0005
Marital status	.0488	-.0658*	-.1015*	-.0344	-.0679*	-.0812*	.0302
Income	.0095	-.0960*	-.1379*	-.0610*	-.0206	.1780*	-.0490
Education	.0836*	-.0934*	-.0704*	.0524*	.0056	.1513*	-.0761*
Occupation	.0331	-.0658*	-.0389	.0351	.0411	.0326	.0090
Multiple correlation coefficient (R)	.3784	.3604	.3460	.3508	.4047	.3560	.2317
Coefficient of determination (R²)	.1432*	.1299*	.1197*	.1231*	.1638*	.1268*	.0537*

[a]For those cases where the coefficient's direction is unclear the following applies: A positive coefficient means that urban residents prefer a particular housing choice more than rural residents (county size and city size); owners prefer it more than renters (tenure status); those presently living in the structure type indicated prefer it more than those who do not (structure type); men prefer it more than women (sex); those married prefer it more than those who are unmarried (marital status); and white-collar workers prefer it more than blue-collar workers (occupation).

* Significant at .001 level.

Relative Effects of Personal Characteristics

To examine the relative effects of the personal characteristics we will focus on each of the other independent variables
according to their placement in the four categories of personal
characteristics: current housing location, current housing
situation, household composition, and social class.   Table 14
shows the results of regressing housing preferences on the personal characteristics.   The first category of personal characteristics is current housing location, and its relationships
with housing preferences are shown in the first two rows in
Table 14.   Neither of the two measures of current housing
location (i.e., county size and city size) have a large effect on
any of the housing preferences.   First, the beta weights for
county size range from .0108 to .0974, with only one reaching
statistical significance (owning a townhouse).   Also, the
direction of the beta weights are not exactly what we would
expect given the bivariate relationships.   For example, a
positive beta weight (b = .0371) exists between county size and
single family home ownership.   We would have predicted a negative relationship--namely, rural residents would prefer single
family home ownership to a greater degree than urban
residents.   Perhaps the most interesting result with regard to
county size is that rural residents tend to prefer the two mobile
home options to a greater extent than urban residents.

The direction of the beta weights for city size and housing
preferences are as expected--positive for the multiple family
dwelling options of renting a duplex, renting an apartment, and
owning a townhouse, and negative for the options involving single family homes and mobile homes.   Again the beta weights are
small, however, ranging from -.0032 to -.0967.   Also, only one
of the beta weights reaches statistical significance (owning a
mobile home and lot).

The regression coefficients presented in Table 14 for the
current housing location variables are similar to the correlation
coefficients reported in Table 10 with regard to directionality.
Only in two instances does the direction of the coefficients
change.   However, there is some change with regard to the
significance of the coefficients.   As reported in Table 10, there
are eight statistically significant correlations between housing
preferences and current housing location.   This compares to
two statistically significant beta weights.   We can conclude,
then, that current housing location has less of an effect on
housing preferences at the multivariate level than at the
bivariate level of analysis.

Thus, city size and county size have little influence on
housing preferences when the effects of the other personal

characteristics in the regression equations are controlled. Only in two cases does current housing location have a significant influence on housing preferences. County size influences preference for owning a townhouse, with urban residents preferring it more than rural residents. City size is important when explaining preference for owning a mobile home and lot, with residents of small communities preferring this housing option to a greater extent than residents of large communities. Of the two variables, city size is slightly more important than county size when examining housing preferences. The beta weights obtained by regressions are larger for city size than for county size in five out of seven instances. However, as previously mentioned, the beta weights are quite low for both measures of current housing location.

The relationships between housing preferences and current housing situation are shown in rows 3-6 in Table 14. Tenure status (own versus rent), the first measure of current housing situation, has little effect on housing preferences. The beta weights range from a low of -.0116 to a high of -.0658. Three of the beta weights are statistically significant. The major finding with regard to tenure status is that all seven beta weights are negative, suggesting that renters prefer all of the housing situations to a greater extent than owners. This finding is rather confusing and difficult to interpret. Perhaps the small size of the beta weights discounts the importance of the directionality. Tenure status appears to influence the options of renting a single family home and renting a duplex to a greater extent than the other options.

Structure type (measured by creating dummy variables for mobile home, single family home, and multiple family home) results in a few relatively strong beta weights. Living in a mobile home is positively related to the two mobile home preferences (b's are .2580 for owning a mobile home and lot, and .1097 for owning a mobile home on rented space) and negatively related to the other options. Four of these beta weights are statistically significant and are larger than .1. Living in a multiple family home is negatively related to the single family home options and positively related to the other choices. However, most of these beta weights are rather small, with only the largest (b = .1692) reaching statistical significance. Living in a single family home is positively related to single family home ownership (b = .1101) and owning a mobile home and lot (b = .0463); it is negatively related to the other options. Three of the beta weights are over .1, and all three are statistically significant.

When the regression coefficients are compared to the correlation coefficients for current housing situation, few major differences emerge.   Directionality changes in only four out of 28 coefficients.   The significance of the coefficients varies to some degree, as 19 of the correlation coefficients are significant compared to only 11 of the regression coefficients.   Thus, the importance of the current housing situation variables is reduced somewhat when they are considered along with the other personal characteristics.   However, the strongest relationships between housing preferences and current housing situation remain the same in the bivariate and multivariate analyses.

Thus, current housing situation has an effect on housing preferences when the other personal characteristics are controlled.   The beta weights for tenure status and structure type are generally larger than those for the current housing location variables.   This suggests that variables reflecting current housing situation have a greater relative influence on housing preferences than those reflecting current housing location. Tenure status is particularly important to consider when explaining preferences for single family home ownership, renting a single family home, and renting a duplex.   However, knowledge of tenure status is not very useful because renters prefer every housing option to a greater extent than owners.   Structure type is more important than tenure status in explaining housing preferences, with current residence in a mobile home having the greatest impact on housing preferences.   In general, current structure type increases the probability of a person preferring that same structure type, with mobile home residents preferring the two mobile home options, those living in multiple family homes preferring the three multiple family home options, and single family home dwellers preferring the options entailing single family homes.

The four indicators of household composition have differential impacts on housing preferences, as shown in rows 7-10 in Table 14.   Household size is negatively related to all the housing situations except the single family home options.   This result coincides with the expectation that large families prefer housing situations providing ample room.   However, the beta weights are not that strong, with the strongest ones being for renting an apartment (b = -.1377) and owning a townhouse (b = -.1050).   Smaller households prefer these housing options to a greater extent than larger households.   Household size has almost no effect on owning a single family home (b = .0055). Four of the beta weights are statistically significant.

Age appears to be a highly significant personal characteristic with regard to explaining housing preferences.   Age is negatively associated with single family home ownership (b = -.2918), renting a single family home (b = -.1444), and owning a townhouse (b = -.0300).   This is consistent with the bivariate relationships, suggesting that older respondents do not want to own their home or to have a large home to the same degree as younger respondents. In fact, the largest beta weight in Table 14 is the one for age and preference for single family home ownership. Age is positively associated with renting an apartment (b = .1857) and owning a mobile home on rented space (b = .1084) to a statistically significant level. Five of the beta weights for age are statistically significant.

The remaining two household composition variables do not have a major impact on housing preferences. Sex has almost no effect on housing preferences, as the beta weights range from .0005 to -.0509. Similarly, marital status has little effect on housing preferences. Only one of the beta weights are over .1 (renting a single family home). The direction of the beta weights for marital status suggest that unmarried respondents prefer housing situations involving multiple family structure type and/or tenancy to a slightly greater extent than married respondents.

There exists a slight difference between the bivariate cor-relation coefficients and the regression coefficients with regard to the importance of the household composition variables. The direction of the coefficients reverses in five instances, three of them when sex is the household composition variable under con-sideration, but these reversals occur for coefficients that are low in both the bivariate and multivariate analyses. The num-ber of statistically significant coefficients varies as well, with only 11 of the beta weights reaching significance compared to 18 of the bivariate correlations. Thus, the importance of the household composition variables is reduced somewhat when they are examined in combination with all the other personal charac-teristics. Overall, however, the household composition variables found to have considerable influence on housing pre-ferences at the bivariate level tend to have a major impact on housing preferences when all other independent variables are controlled.

Comparing the size and statistical significance of the beta weights obtained by the household composition variables to those obtained by current housing location and current housing situation, it appears that the household composition variables have the greatest relative impact on housing preferences. The two variables of household size and age, in particular, have strong independent effects on housing preferences. It seems clear that large households prefer single family homes over the options entailing less space, and older respondents prefer hous-ing situations involving tenancy rather than ownership. Thus knowledge of these two household composition variables in-creases our ability to predict housing preferences. Sex and marital status are not nearly as important to consider, but the latter personal characteristic does influence housing preferences to a slight extent.

The three indicators of social class also have differential impacts on housing preferences. The relationships between social class and housing preferences are shown in rows 11-13 in Table 14. Income produces four statistically significant beta weights, with two of them exceeding .1. Income is positively associated with the preferences of owning a single family home, renting an apartment, and owning a townhouse. The relationship between income and preference for owning a townhouse is particularly substantial (b = .1780). It is negatively related to the other options, although the beta weights are rather small with only one exception (b = -.1379 for renting a single family home).

Education, the second measure of social class, is a slightly better predictor of housing preferences than income. The beta weights range from a low of .0056 to a high of .1513. Six of the beta weights are statistically significant. The strongest relationship is between owning a townhouse and education (b = .1513). Education is negatively associated with the two mobile home options (b = -.0934 for owning a mobile home and lot; b = -.0761 for owning a mobile home on rented space). It is positively related to the remaining choices.

Occupation is the poorest of the three social class variables in terms of predicting housing preferences. The beta weights are small (ranging from .0090 to -.0658) and only one is statistically significant at the .001 level. Occupation is positively associated with all of the housing options with the exception of renting a single family home (b = -.0389) and owning a mobile home and lot (b = -.0658). The latter statistic is rather significant, as it suggests that owning a mobile home and lot is preferred more by blue-collar workers than by white-collar workers.

Comparing the regression coefficients for the social class variables shown in Table 14 with the correlation coefficients presented in Table 10 reveals a few differences. Directionality changes in two instances, one of them being rather significant. At the bivariate level income is negatively associated with preference for renting an apartment while at the multivariate level it is positively associated with that preference. The significance of the coefficients is fairly consistent, with 14 of the correlation coefficients being statistically significant and 11 of the beta weights being statistically significant. There is one important change with regard to which of the social class variables has the greatest relative impact on housing preferences. At the bivariate level income appears to have the greatest impact on housing preferences; however, after controlling for other personal characteristics education appears to be the most important social class variable to consider when predicting housing preferences.

Thus, social class has a definite impact on housing preferences when controlling for the other personal characteristics in the various regression equations. Although occupation has a significant impact only on preference for owning a mobile home and lot, which is preferred to a greater extent by blue-collar workers than white-collar workers, income and education influence several of the housing preferences. Income is particularly crucial when explaining preferences for owning a mobile home and lot, renting a single family home, renting a duplex, and owning a townhouse. Education has an independent effect on all of the preferences with the exception of one--renting an apartment. Not surprisingly, people in the lower social classes, as indicated by low income, low education, and low occupational prestige, are more likely to prefer mobile homes, while those in the higher social classes tend to prefer single family home ownership. In comparison with the other categories of personal characteristics, the social class category is similar to household composition in terms of the number of significant coefficients, although the magnitudes tend to be lower.

Cumulative Effects of Personal Characteristics

Before summarizing the relative effects of the various personal characteristics on housing preferences, we will examine the amount of variation in the dependent variables that is explained by all 11 independent variables. The bottom row of Table 14 shows the total amount of explained variation (R^2) obtained by regressing housing preferences on all 11 personal characteristics. The R^2's range from a low of .0537 (owning a mobile home on rented space) to a high of .1638 (renting an apartment). This means that we can explain between approximately 5 percent and 16 percent of the variation in the various housing preferences. All but one of the R^2's is above .10, so we can explain at least 10 percent of the variation in six of the seven housing preferences. The sizes of the R^2's suggest several things. First, knowledge of personal characteristics does not allow us to predict housing preferences very well. Secondly, personal characteristics still have some influence on housing preferences and should be considered in housing preference research. Further, it appears that personal characteristics have a greater impact on some housing preferences (e.g., renting an apartment) than on other housing preferences (e.g., owning a mobile home on rented space). With regard to certain

housing preferences, then, personal characteristics are especially important to consider.

While it is useful to know the total variation in housing
preferences explained by personal characteristics, we still do
not have a good idea of how the various categories of personal
characteristics contribute to that variation. In Table 15 we
show the explained variation in housing preferences for the
four stages of the regression equations, starting with current
housing location and then adding current housing situation,
household composition, and social class, in that order. This allows us to examine the amount of variation each category of
personal characteristics adds to the total explained variation.
To obtain these results we first regressed the housing preferences on the current housing location variables, then added the
current housing situation variables to the regression equation,
followed by the household composition variables and, finally,
the social class variables.

Usually there is a theoretical rationale for deciding the
order in which the independent variables are placed in the
regression equations. Unfortunately, there is no past research
on housing preferences which suggests any type of order.
However, the order of the independent variables selected here
does have some justification. An examination of the correlation
coefficients and regression coefficients indicates that current
housing location and current housing situation have the weakest
influence on housing preferences. Thus, they are ordered first
and second in the regression equations so that a good deal of
the variation should be left unexplained by these two groups of
personal characteristics. Further, by placing these two categories of personal characteristics in the initial two stages of the
regression equation their effects are taken into account when
we turn to the more theoretically interesting categories of
household composition and social class. Since the social class
variables have played a particularly prominent role in the mass
society perspective, it seems appropriate to consider these variables after household composition. Thus, household composition
is ordered third and social class is ordered fourth in the regression equations. In fact, placing social class last in the
regression equations provides the strongest possible test of the
utility of the class-differential values hypothesis versus the
class-consensus values hypothesis (the basis of our formulation
of the differential housing preference hypothesis and the consensus housing preference hypothesis).

The first row in Table 15 shows the R^2's for the
regression of each housing preference on the current housing
location variables of county size and city size. These two
variables account for a high of 3.0 percent of the variation in

Table 15. Summary of the Explained Variation (R^2) Obtained by the Regression Equations Predicting Housing Preferences by Four Categories of Personal Characteristics

Categories of Personal Characteristics	Housing Preferences						
	Buy Single Family House	Buy Mobile Home and Lot	Rent Single Family House	Rent Duplex	Rent Apartment	Buy Townhouse	Buy Mobile Home on Rented Space
Current housing location	.0030	.0267	.0013	.0088	.0129	.0300	.0013
Current housing situation	.0371	.0936	.0633	.0944	.0891	.0498	.0234
Household composition	.1326	.0974	.1039	.1177	.1612	.0586	.0452
Social class	.1432	.1299	.1197	.1231	.1638	.1268	.0537

preference for owning a townhouse and 2.7 percent of the variation in preference for owning a mobile home and lot. The lowest amount of variation explained by current housing location occurs for the preferences of renting a single family home and owning a mobile home on rented space (.1 percent). Although there is some difference in the amount of variation explained by current housing location, it is low in every instance. Thus, current housing location accounts for very little of the variation in any of the seven housing preferences.

The second row in Table 15 shows the R^2's for the regressions obtained with the addition of the current housing situation variables of tenure status and structure type. The difference between row 2 and row 1 is the variation explained by current housing situation over that explained by current housing location. In examining these differences, the table shows that current housing situation adds between 2.0 percent (owning a townhouse) and 8.6 percent (renting a duplex) to the variation explained by current housing location. Thus, current housing situation substantially increases the R^2 for several of the housing preferences. The largest increases occur in the preferences of renting a duplex, renting an apartment, owning a mobile home and lot, and renting a single family home. Current housing situation, therefore, has considerable influence on four of the housing preferences, while adding very little to the remaining three housing preferences. However, most of this variation is explained by structure type. This finding supports our earlier conclusion--namely, people tend to prefer housing situations entailing the same structure type as their current home.

The third row shows the R^2's obtained after the household composition variables of household size, age, sex, and marital status are included in the regression equations. The difference between this row and row 2 is the additional variation explained by household composition after current housing location and current housing situation are considered. Household composition adds very little to the variation explained in the preferences of owning a townhouse, owning a mobile home on rented space, renting a duplex, and owning a mobile home and lot. However, it substantially increases the R^2 for owning a single family home, renting an apartment, and renting a single family home. The amount of variation explained by household composition after taking current housing location and current housing situation into account ranges from a low of .4 percent (owning a mobile home and lot) to a high of 9.6 percent (owning a single family home). Thus, household composition has a substantial effect on some of the housing preferences. This finding should not be surprising given our earlier discussion:

differences in household composition lead to the need for housing situations satisfying differing demands.

Finally, the last row displays the R^2's for the complete regression equations (identical to the multiple coefficients of determination presented in Table 14), as the social class variables of income, education, and occupation are included along with the other personal characteristics. Thus, the difference between row 3 and row 4 is the additional explained variation attributable to social class. Social class adds between .3 percent of the variation in preference for renting an apartment and 6.8 percent of the variation in owning a townhouse. Social class has the largest impact on the preferences of owning a townhouse (R^2 increases from .0586 to .1268) and owning a mobile home and lot (R^2 increases from .0974 to .1299), while having very little impact on the remaining five housing preferences. Overall, the social class variables do not explain much variation once the other personal characteristics are taken into account. This suggests that once people's current housing situation and the composition of their household is considered, their social class characteristics do not have a major impact on their housing preferences.

RECAPITULATION AND DISCUSSION

To clarify the influence of personal characteristics on housing preferences, it was decided to conduct a multivariate analysis. Employing this type of analysis allows us to examine the relative and cumulative effects that personal characteristics have on housing preferences. It is revealed that in terms of relative effects, the personal characteristics differ with regard to their influence on housing preferences. Based on the size and significance of the standardized regression coefficients, structure type, household size, age, income, and education appear to be the most important personal characteristics when attempting to explain housing preferences. In terms of the general personal characteristic categories, the current housing situation variables and the household composition variables have the greatest impact on housing preferences, the social class variables have some impact, and the current housing location variables have very little impact.

However, it is important to note that none of the personal characteristics has a consistently strong effect on all seven housing preferences. In fact, when explaining a specific housing preference different personal characteristics are important to consider. For example, the variables of tenure status, single family structure type, age, and education are the important ones to consider when examining the preference for single family home ownership. On the other hand, the variables of multiunit structure type, household size, age, and marital status are the important ones to consider when examining the preference for renting an apartment. This suggests that different personal characteristics must be considered depending upon the housing preference under study.

Although the personal characteristics do differ in terms of their relative importance with regard to predicting housing preferences, none of them appear to be consistently strong predictors of these preferences. For example, age has a substantial impact on some of the housing preferences. On the other hand, characteristics such as sex have little impact on any of the housing preferences.

The cumulative effects of the personal characteristics on housing preferences are fairly small. The 11 personal characteristics together explain a total of from 5 percent (owning a mobile home on rented space) to 16 percent (renting an apartment) of the variation in housing preferences. Thus, even though they have some effect, personal characteristics do not appear to be a substantial factor in determining housing preferences. This conclusion casts some doubt on the utility of the differential housing preference hypothesis. On the one hand, the results do provide weak support for the differential housing preference hypothesis, as housing preferences vary to some extent based on personal characteristics. On the other hand, these differences are not large ones.

6

Housing at the Crossroad

We are entering a new housing era. The assumption that the vast majority of Americans will own a conventional single family detached house will be seriously questioned as housing prices increase and resources upon which housing is dependent decrease. Many families are already confronting the rapidly changing housing situation, and are deciding to live in alternative housing forms. More families will most likely join their ranks in the years to come.

OVERVIEW OF RESULTS

The purpose of this book has been to provide a broad overview of the acceptability of an array of housing alternatives now available to the American public. We have focused on the examination of housing preferences, which connote the kinds of housing situations in which people do and do not want to live. Seven housing situations considered to be readily available to Americans were measured regarding the extent to which they are preferred: owning a single family home, owning a mobile home and lot, renting a single family home, owning a townhouse, renting a duplex, renting an apartment, and owning a mobile home on rented space.

By extensively reviewing previous research on housing preferences and analyzing housing preference data collected from a statewide survey we can draw three important conclusions. These conclusions provide insights regarding the types of homes in which Americans may live in the future.

First, ownership of a conventional single family detached home is the preferred housing situation by an overwhelming majority. Interest in all other possibilities is relatively low, with the number two choice being owning a mobile home and lot and the number three choice being renting a single family home. The remaining housing situations receive very low levels of support. Thus, the prevailing assumption that the majority of Americans want to own a conventional single family detached home still holds true. Any attempts to block Americans from obtaining their preferred housing situation will most likely be actively resisted.

Second, housing preferences can be at least partially explained by a consideration of four housing norms: home ownership, single family detached dwelling, private outside space, and conventional construction. These norms prescribe the housing situations in which Americans ought to live, and are supported by social rewards for conformity to the norms and social punishments for nonconformity to the norms. Generally, housing situations are preferred to a greater or lesser extent based on how closely they satisfy various housing norms. Owning a conventional single family detached home is the preferred housing choice because it satisfies all four norms, while the other six housing situations are preferred to lesser extents depending upon how many norms they fail to satisfy.

If the most preferred housing situation is not attainable, people substitute a housing situation which most closely satisfies a similar number and similar kinds of norms as met by their first preference. When people cannot obtain ownership of a conventional single family detached home, they tend to select owning a mobile home and lot (loss of conventionality) or renting a single family home (loss of ownership) which both satisfy three norms. Therefore, if ownership of a conventional single family detached home becomes problematic in the future, we can expect certain types of alternative housing to be relatively acceptable based on knowledge of the four housing norms.

Finally, personal characteristics of respondents influence housing preferences to some extent. The personal characteristics of structure type, household size, age, income, and education have the greatest impact on housing preferences; however, none of these characteristics has a consistently strong effect on housing preferences. When all of the personal characteristics assessed in our study are considered as a whole, they explain only between 5 percent and 16 percent of the variation in housing preferences. On the one hand, it appears that the social factors of mass media, observation, economics, prestige, and symbol of self minimize differences in housing preferences. On the other hand, those differences which do exist result from unequal internalization of the norms based on people's unique life circumstances.

RECOMMENDATIONS FOR FURTHER STUDY

Although the survey upon which this book is based corrected certain deficiencies contained in previous studies on housing preferences, some problems remain. First, the mail questionnaire is used as the method for obtaining knowledge of housing preferences. Future research might employ different methods to assess housing preferences so that the results across study methods can be compared. Second, one option not explicitly considered in this study needs to be extensively researched in the future--namely, condominiums. By combining a variety of housing structure types with the tenure status of ownership, it would be possible to accurately measure preferences regarding condominiums. Finally, we have data for only one state. Thus, there may be some geographical bias in the results obtained. It is necessary to obtain knowledge of the housing preferences of people residing in a variety of states. A national survey on housing preferences would provide the most reliable information regarding the housing preferences of Americans. These shortcomings of our study should be corrected by future research efforts.

Given the importance of housing norms in understanding housing preferences, it is crucial that further research be conducted on this topic. One avenue of research is to identify all of the housing norms. There exist several possible housing norms not considered in this study (e.g., number of bedrooms, size of home, and number of bathrooms) which need to be identified and studied with regard to housing preferences. Another avenue of research is to order the four housing norms according to their strength. We have no direct evidence concerning which of the norms is most important to Americans. If the norms can be ordered in terms of their strength, it would allow us to better predict housing preferences. This is especially true of people's second housing preference. Future research might reveal a norm which most people would part with first, meaning that they would find a housing situation satisfying the other three housing norms acceptable. For example, we might find that if people cannot afford ownership of a conventional single family detached house, many will part with the norm of detached single family home and buy a townhouse unit. Research on housing norms will greatly aid efforts to understand where Americans will live.

There are some problems with our analysis of the relationships between housing preferences and personal characteristics which need to be corrected by future research. A more detailed account of the differential housing preference hypothesis and the consensus housing preference hypothesis needs to be given. These two hypotheses have significant theoretical implications for housing preference research. A greater number of personal characteristics might be subjected to study in future research. Given the low amount of explained variation in housing preferences accounted for by our 11 personal characteristics, we wonder whether some other important personal characteristics exist (e.g., race and childhood residence). Since the multivariate analysis conducted in Chapter 5 only took into account the dependent variables measuring the extent to which people would consider living in each housing situation, it would be useful to conduct such an analysis on the dependent variables measuring combined first and second preferences as well. Finally, a more sophisticated analysis indicating the direct and indirect effects of the personal characteristics on housing preferences needs to be conducted. This would allow us to better identify the personal characteristics which are most crucial to consider when explaining housing preferences.

Our major concern is that there is some question whether Americans will have access to conventional single family detached home ownership in the future. If it is true that the majority of people prefer this housing situation, many Americans will be frustrated with the homes available to them (e.g., mobile homes and apartments). Thus, further research on housing preferences is essential. There is also a need to systematically measure trends affecting housing in American society. Future research in this area might develop indicators of housing costs as well as indicators of the supply of resources needed for housing construction. Another possible research endeavor is to further investigate the relationship between housing and total life satisfaction. Policymakers might begin considering how to deal with people frustrated with their housing situation, and how to assist Americans in obtaining the best possible housing given extant societal constraints. In short, we need a more systematic way to measure housing trends and the way in which they affect people's lives.

OUR FUTURE HOUSING

To move from preference data to actual policy decisions requires taking some very large steps, and we do not wish to unrealistically simplify the connection. Our own position is that policy decisions must incorporate useful information derived from a variety of sources. Since housing preferences reflect predispositions to act in particular ways and indicate what kinds of homes people will find acceptable, we feel that they are an important source of information for policy decision-makers. Although housing preferences are only one consideration in the making of housing policy, some tentative conclusions with policy relevance do emerge from the findings.

The most significant conclusion is that there is no heir apparent waiting in the wings to replace the owned conventional single family detached dwelling, and for policymakers to assume there is, on the basis of people's preferences, would be a mistake. Although several housing environments are acceptable to some extent by people if they cannot attain conventional single family detached home ownership, none of the alternatives has consensus. Rather, acceptability of the alternatives varies according to what segment of the population is under consideration. Thus, it would be a mistake to think in terms of formulating a uniform housing policy that emphasizes only one of the alternative housing situations. It seems clear that policymakers need to develop housing policies which are flexible enough to deal with the preferences of several different segments of the population.

Where will Americans live? Based on stated housing preferences, the obvious answer is conventional single family detached homes which are owned. This housing situation has been regarded as a goal of Americans since the nation's founding. However, rising housing costs and shortages of certain housing resources cast a shadow over the realization of this goal. A substantial number of families will not be financially capable of purchasing a conventional single family detached home in the future. Even those able to afford their preferred housing situation may find that there exists an acute shortage of conventional single family detached homes for sale because of land shortages or the expense of providing community services. If this is an accurate picture of things to come, in what kinds of homes will Americans live? We believe there are three major possibilities.

First, a growing number of Americans will most likely live in multiple family dwellings such as apartments, duplexes, and townhouses. These housing options require less energy, less land, fewer building materials, and fewer community services per housing unit than conventional single family detached homes. They are also less expensive to purchase if such an option exists. Throughout our nation's history many Americans have lived in multiple family dwellings, but most people have considered them as a short-term housing solution. As people form families and begin earning respectable incomes they traditionally leave the multiple family dwelling for ownership of a conventional single family detached home. To convince Americans that life in multiple family dwellings may be a permanent housing situation will not be an easy task.

Results from our housing preference survey show that owning a townhouse is the most preferred multiple family dwelling option, followed by renting a duplex and renting an apartment. Thus, ownership of a townhouse unit might be acceptable to many Americans, particularly those with high income and education levels, with small family sizes, and who reside in urban areas. As our society becomes more urbanized, better educated, and dominated by families with one or perhaps two children it is likely that preferences directed at multiple family dwellings will increase.

However, the multiple family dwellings which are typically viewed as undesirable by Americans will take on a very different look. Even if people cannot purchase a conventional single family detached home, they will still want their housing to satisfy as many of the four housing norms as possible. Those people deciding to live in multiple family dwellings will attempt to obtain home ownership, private outside space, and conventional structure type even though they will lose the attribute of detached single family dwelling. Condominium ownership of a townhouse unit which includes ownership of the land immediately surrounding the dwelling unit, perhaps by shrubs or a small fence, may be the solution to this group of Americans. Duplexes and apartments can satisfy the same three housing norms, although private outside space for apartment dwellers may mean a private patio or deck.

Besides the provision of three of the housing norms, a great deal can be done to increase the acceptability of multiple family dwellings. The placement of these housing units in desirable community locations is probably the most important improvement. Attractive landscaping and the inclusion of recreational facilities would attract more people to multiple family dwellings. The use of building materials to minimize noise between adjoining unit walls and taking advantage of interior design techniques to maximize space usage would also enhance the image of multiple family homes.

A second possibility consists of mobile homes. The mobile home industry has experienced rapid growth over the past decade with no end to such growth expected. Mobile homes are considered as acceptable housing particularly by those with low education and income levels, who are either young or old, and who live in rural areas. Mobile homes are increasingly being selected by the elderly for retirement housing and by young families who cannot afford a conventional single family detached home.

There exist several problems with mobile homes which must be reduced if this housing option is to be accepted by many

Americans. Foremost among these problems are zoning ordinances, construction specifications, and mortgage interest rates. Zoning ordinances typically relegate mobile homes to the court or park setting located in less desirable neighborhood surroundings. Construction specifications have been lax, allowing the production of mobile homes meeting only minimal safety requirements. Purchasers of mobile homes are typically subjected to shorter term mortgages at higher interest rates than is true for conventional single family detached homes. Changes in zoning ordinances which allow mobile homes to be located in desirable locations, construction specifications which ensure safety, and mortgages which are similar to those provided for conventional single family detached homes would increase the acceptability of mobile homes.

Our preference data reveal a major difference in acceptability between mobile homes located on rented space in a mobile home park and mobile homes which are placed on private lots. Owning a mobile home and lot, in fact, was the number two preference of our respondents. This suggests that mobile homes on privately owned lots lack much of the social stigma traditionally ascribed to those located on rented space in mobile home parks. Mobile homes gain permanence, if not a sense of status, when they are placed on permanent foundations and become defined by the tax assessor as real property.

Those deciding to live in mobile homes will give up the norm of conventional construction but can still obtain home ownership, private outside space, and detached single family dwelling. With the suggested changes mentioned above, more people will view mobile homes as acceptable. The emergence of well-designed mobile home parks where people own their home and the land surrounding it and the increased scattering of mobile homes placed on permanent foundations in rural areas may become desirable housing options for many families.

Finally, it will remain possible for some Americans to purchase conventional single family detached homes. Of course there are always some families with the financial resources to buy whatever they want, and they will continue to purchase conventional single family detached homes. For many others, the dream of the "typical" conventional single family detached home with four bedrooms, two bathrooms, fireplace, and a large yard will become less realistic given societal constraints. This means that conventional single family detached homes will still be purchased, but they will most likely be smaller and built of cheaper materials.

Over the next decade, a conventional single family detached home will probably decline from an average size of

1,600 square feet to perhaps 1,000 square feet. A decrease in size will reduce the price of conventional single family detached homes as well as make more efficient use of building materials, land, and energy for cooling and heating. To minimize the effects of reduced size architects, builders, and interior designers will be required to provide the impression of space. The creative use of windows, skylights, colors, room arrangements, and furnishings will increase the attractiveness of smaller homes.

Conventional single family detached homes will most likely be built with less expensive materials in the future. The use of carbon and boron materials may achieve the look of brick or aluminum siding at a much lower cost. Plastic may appear in more window frames, exterior trim, and pipes. Wood products made from scrap might be commonly used in housing construction. It is quite possible that cost reduction efforts will lead in the direction of more factory built materials, perhaps even wall sections and complete rooms, blurring the norm of conventional structure type.

Conventional single family detached homes of the future will be made more energy efficient through the use of a variety of methods. Installation of heavy insulation, weatherstripping, caulking, and interior design adaptations will increase the energy efficiency of homes. It is probable that earth-sheltered and solar homes will become more prevalent. These changes will reduce energy costs which are already reaching high levels and creating a financial burden for many families.

Given the strong preference for ownership of a conventional single family detached home among Americans, many people will make major sacrifices to obtain their preferred housing situation. Size reductions, the use of cheaper building materials, and increased energy efficiency may keep the cost of conventional single family detached homes low enough so this housing situation remains a viable option to many American families.

One thing is clear. We are now entering a new housing era in the United States. It will be an era much like that faced by the automobile industry in recent years, where cars have been reduced in size, made more energy efficient, and built of cheaper and fewer materials. The precise nature of the new housing era cannot be accurately predicted at this time; only the future will tell if our "dream house" will become as obsolete as an oversized Cadillac. However, knowledge of people's housing preferences can aid our efforts to understand our future housing.

References

Aaron, Henry
  1972   Shelter and Subsidies: Who Benefits from Federal Housing Policies? Washington, D.C.: Brookings Institution.

Abrams, Charles
  1946   The Future of Housing. New York: Harper.

Anderson, Martin
  1964   The Federal Bulldozer: A Critical Analysis of Urban Renewal, 1947-1962. Cambridge, MA: MIT Press.

Andrews, Frank M., and Stephen B. Withey
  1976   Social Indicators of Well-Being. New York: Plenum.

Angell, William J.
  1978   Incidence of Fire and Wind Damage and Destruction of Mobile Homes and Single-Family Dwellings. St. Paul: Agricultural Extension Service, University of Minnesota.

Angell, William J.
  1979   "Housing alternatives." Pp. 245-278 in C. S. Wedin and L. G. Nygren (eds.), Housing Perspectives. Minneapolis: Burgess.

Automation in Housing
  1980   "Industrialized/manufactured housing virtually matches 1978 in 1979." Automation in Housing 17:20-22.

Barlowe, Raleigh
  1979   "Land for housing." Pp. 56-77 in C. S. Wedin and L. G. Nygren (eds.), Housing Perspectives. Minneapolis: Burgess.

Becker, Franklin D.
  1974   Design for Living: The Residents' View of Multi-Family Housing. Ithaca, NY: Center for Urban Development Research, Cornell University.

Belcher, John C.
  1970   "Differential aspirations for housing between blacks and whites in rural Georgia." Phylon 31:231-243.

Beyer, Glenn H.
  1965   Housing and Society. New York: Macmillan.

Bierstedt, Robert
    1963   The Social Order. New York: McGraw-Hill.

Bird, Ronald, and Ronald Kampe
    1977   25 Years of Housing Progress in Rural America.
            Washington, D.C.: U.S. Department of Agriculture,
            Agricultural Economic Report No. 373.

Black, Judith, and Kingsley Davis
    1964   "Norms, values and sanctions." Pp. 456-484 in R. E.
            L. Faris (ed.), Handbook of Modern Sociology.
            Chicago: Rand McNally.

Booth, Allan
    1976   Urban Crowding and Its Consequences. New York:
            Praeger.

Boulding, Kenneth
    1956   The Image. Ann Arbor: University of Michigan
            Press.

Branch, M. C., Jr.
    1942   Urban Planning and Public Opinion. Princeton, NJ:
            Bureau of Urban Research, Princeton University.

Breckenfeld, Gurney
    1976   "Is the one-family house becoming a fossil? Far from
            it." Fortune 93 (April):84-89, 164-165.

Brunsman, Howard G.
    1947   "Current sources of sociological data in housing."
            American Sociological Review 12:150-155.

Bureau of Vital Statistics
    1976   Vital Statistics, 1975. Olympia, WA: Washington
            State Department of Social and Health Services.

Campbell, Angus, Phillip E. Converse, and Willard L. Rodgers
    1976   The Quality of American Life. New York: Russell
            Sage Foundation.

Canter, David, and Ross Thorne
    1972   "Attitudes to housing: A cross-cultural comparison."
            Environment and Behavior 4:3-32.

Caplow, Theodore
    1948   "Home ownership and location preferences in a
            Minneapolis sample." American Sociological Review
            13:725-730.

Carlton, Dennis W., and Joseph Ferreira, Jr.
  1977   "Selecting subsidy strategies for housing allowance programs." Journal of Urban Economics 4:221-247.

Carpenter, Edwin H.
  1977   "Evaluation of mail questionnaires for obtaining data from more than one respondent in a household." Rural Sociology 42:250-259.

Chapin, F. Stuart
  1947   "New methods of sociological research on housing problems." American Sociological Review 12:143-149.

Clapperton, R. Ian, and Joseph Carreiro
  1972   "Innovations in technology: Mobile home and modular housing." Ithaca, NY: Department of Design and Environmental Analysis, Cornell University.

Cleere, Ford W.
  1979   "Mobile homes: The proletarianization of the American dream." Paper presented at the annual meeting of the Pacific Sociological Association, Anaheim, CA.

Cloward, Richard A., and Lloyd E. Ohlin
  1960   Delinquency and Opportunity. New York: Free Press.

Cohen, J. B., and A. W. Hansen
  1972   Personal Finance. Homewood, IL: Irwin.

Coons, A. E., and B. T. Glaze
  1963   Housing Market Analysis and the Growth of Nonfarm Home Ownership. Columbus, OH: Bureau of Business Research, Ohio State University.

Cooper, Clare C.
  1972   "The house as symbol." Design and Environment 3: 30-37.

Cooper, Clare C.
  1975   Easter Hill Village: Some Social Implications of Design. New York: Free Press.

Davis, Allison
  1946   "The motivation of the underprivileged worker." Pp. 84-106 in W. F. Whyte (ed.), Industry and Society. New York: McGraw-Hill.

Dean, John P.
1953 "Housing design and family values." Land Economics 29: 128-141.

Dillman, Don A.
1978 Mail and Telephone Surveys: The Total Design Method. New York: Wiley-Interscience.

Dillman, Don A., and Kenneth R. Tremblay, Jr.
1977 "The quality of life in rural America." Annals of the American Academy of Political and Social Science 429: 115-129.

Dillman, Joye J., Kenneth R. Tremblay, Jr., and Don A. Dillman
1977 "Energy policies directed at the home: Which ones will people accept?" Housing Educators Journal 4: 2-13.

Downs, Anthony
1974 "The successes and failures of federal housing policy." The Public Interest 34:124-145.

Dubos, Rene
1968 So Human An Animal. New York: Charles Scribner's Sons.

Duhl, Leonard J. (ed.)
1963 The Urban Condition: People and Policy in the Metropolis. New York: Simon and Schuster.

Dunlap, Riley E., and William R. Catton, Jr.
1979 "Environmental Sociology." Annual Review of Sociology 5:243-273.

Egan, Richard
1977 "House buying: The myths and the facts." National Observer (Jan. 1):9.

Fave, L. Richard Della
1974 "Success values: Are they universal or class-differentiated?" American Journal of Sociology 80: 153-169.

Federal National Mortgage Association
1982 Buying a Home in the Eighties. Washington, D.C.: Federal National Mortgage Association.

Fischer, Claude S.
  1975   "Toward a subcultural theory of urbanism." American
          Journal of Sociology 80:1319-1341.

Freedman, R.
  1968   "Norms for family size in underdeveloped areas."
          Pp. 215-230 in C. B. Nam (ed.), Population and
          Society. Boston: Houghton-Mifflin.

Gans, Herbert J.
  1965   "The failure of urban renewal." Commentary 39:
          29-37.

Gelwicks, Louis E., and Robert J. Newcomer
  1974   Planning Housing Environments for the Elderly.
          Washington, D.C.: National Council on the Aging.

Gerardie, Natalie
  1976   "A new survey from a trend-setting market: What
          single-family buyers want." Los Angeles: Unpub-
          lished paper.

Gibbs, Jack P.
  1965   "Norms: The problem of definition and classifica-
          tion." American Journal of Sociology 70:586-594.

Gibbs, Jack P.
  1978   "Norms and normative properties." Pp. 140-150 in
          E. Sagarin (ed.), Sociology: The Basic Concepts.
          New York: Holt, Rinehart and Winston.

Goffman, Erving
  1959   The Presentation of Self in Everyday Life. Garden
          City, NY: Doubleday.

Golant, Stephen M.
  1977   "The housing tenure adjustments of the young and
          the elderly: Policy implications." Urban Affairs
          Quarterly 13:95-108.

Goudy, Willis J.
  1978   "Interim response to a mail questionnaire." Sociologi-
          cal Quarterly 19:253-265.

Gove, Walter R., James W. Grimm, Susan C. Motz, and J. D.
Thompson
  1973   "The family life cycle." Sociology and Social
          Research 57:182-195.

Greendale, Alexander, and Stanley F. Knock, Jr. (eds.)
    1976   Housing Costs and Housing Needs. New York:
            Praeger.

Grier, George W.
    1967   "Negro ghettos and federal housing policy." Law and
            Contemporary Problems 32:550-560.

Grimes, Orville, F., Jr.
    1976   Housing for Low-Income Urban Families. Baltimore,
            MD: Johns Hopkins University Press.

Gutman, Robert
    1970   "A sociologist looks at housing." Pp. 119-132 in
            D. P. Moynihan (ed.), Toward a National Urban
            Policy. New York: Basic.

Hamilton, R. E.
    1966   "The marginal middle class." American Sociological
            Review 31:192-199.

Han, Wan Sang
    1969   "Two conflicting themes: Common values versus class
            differential values." American Sociological Review
            34:679-690.

Hanna, Sherman, and Suzanne Lindamood
    1979   "Housing preferences of blacks and whites in
            Montgomery, Alabama." Housing and Society 6:39-47.

Hartman, Chester
    1963   "Social values and housing orientations." Journal of
            Social Issues 19:113-131.

Hartman, Chester W.
    1975   Housing and Social Policy. Englewood Cliffs, NJ:
            Prentice-Hall.

Hawkins, Homer C.
    1976   "Urban housing and the black family." Phylon 37:
            73-84.

Heimstra, Norman W., and Leslie H. McFarling
    1978   Environmental Psychology. Monterey, CA: Brooks/
            Cole.

Hinshaw, Mark, and Kathryn Allott
    1972   "Environmental preferences of future housing con-
            sumers." Journal of the American Institute of Plan-
            ners 38:102-107.

Hoben, James E.
    1975   "The costs of sprawl." HUD Challenge (January):24-26.

Homans, George C.
    1961   Social Behavior: Its Elementary Forms. New York: Harcourt, Brace and World.

Huttman, Elizabeth D.
    1977   Housing and Social Services for the Elderly: Some Policy Trends. New York: Praeger.

Hyman, Herbert H.
    1963   "The value systems of different classes." Pp. 426-442 in R. Bendix and S. M. Lipset (eds.), Class, Status and Power. New York: Free Press.

Kelly, S., and T. W. Mirer
    1974   "The simple act of voting." American Political Science Review 68:572-591.

Kerlinger, Fred N., and Elazar J. Pedhazur
    1973   Multiple Regression in Behavioral Research. New York: Holt, Rinehart and Winston.

Kushell, Elliot
    1977   "Notes on the concept of 'significant environment' and its application to public housing problems." Paper presented at the annual meeting of the Pacific Sociological Association, Sacramento, CA.

Ladd, Florence C.
    1972   "Black youths view their environments: Some views of housing." Journal of the American Institute of Planners 38:108-116.

Lakshmanan, T. R., Lata Chatterjee, and P. Roy
    1976   "Housing requirements and national resources." Science 192:943-949.

Lansing, J. B., E. Mueller, and N. Barth
    1964   Residential Location and Urban Mobility. Ann Arbor: Institute for Social Research, University of Michigan.

Lazin, Frederick A.
    1976   "Federal low-income housing assistance programs and racial segregation: Leased public housing." Public Policy 24:337-360.

Lennard, Suzanne H. Crownhurst, and Henry L. Lennard
    1977   "Architecture: Effect of territory, boundary, and
            orientation on family functioning." Family Process
            16:49-66.

Lindamood, Suzanne
    1974   "Housing as a process." Housing Educators Journal
            1:22-28.

Lindamood, Suzanne, and Sherman D. Hanna
    1979   Housing, Society and Consumers. St. Paul: West.

Loo, Chalsa M.
    1978   "Behavior problem indices: The differential effects of
            spatial density on low and high scorers." Environ-
            ment and Behavior 10:489-510.

Lord, Tom Forrester
    1977   Decent Housing: A Promise to Keep. Cambridge,
            MA: Schenkman.

Manvel, A. D.
    1968   Housing Conditions in Urban Poverty Areas.
            Washington, D.C.: U.S. Government Printing Office.

McCray, Jacquelyn W., and Savannah S. Day
    1977   "Housing values, aspirations, and satisfaction as indi-
            cators of housing needs." Home Economics Research
            Journal 5:244-254.

McKown, Cora
    1975   "Social factors related to housing selection." Housing
            Educators Journal 2:11-16.

Meehan, Eugene J.
    1975   Public Housing Policy. New Brunswick, NJ: Rutgers
            University Press.

Merton, Robert K.
    1948   "The social psychology of housing." Pp. 163-217 in
            W. Dennis (ed.), Current Trends in Social Psychol-
            ogy. Pittsburgh: University of Pittsburgh Press.

Merton, Robert K.
    1957   Social Theory and Social Structure. New York: Free
            Press.

Meyerson, Martin, Barbara Terrett, and William Wheaton
    1962   Housing, People and Cities. New York:
            McGraw-Hill.

Michelson, William
    1966   "An empirical analysis of urban environment prefer-
            ences." Journal of the American Institute of Planners
            32:355-360.

Michelson, William
    1967   "Potential candidates for the designer's paradise: A
            social analysis from a nationwide survey."   Social
            Forces 46:190-196.

Michelson, William
    1968   "Most people don't want what architects want."
            Transaction 5:37-43.

Michelson, William
    1976   Man and His Urban Environment: A Sociological
            Approach.   Reading, MA: Addison-Wesley.

Michelson, William
    1977   Environmental Choice, Human Behavior, and Residen-
            tial Satisfaction.   New York: Oxford University
            Press.

Miller, Walter B.
    1958   "Lower class culture as generating milieu of gang
            delinquency."   Journal of Social Issues 14:5-19.

Mitchell, Robert E.
    1974   "Misconceptions about man-made space: In partial
            defense of high density housing."   The Family
            Coordinator 22:51-56.

Montgomery, James E.
    1970   "Impact of housing patterns on marital interaction."
            The Family Coordinator 19:267-275.

Montgomery, James E., and Joseph E. Kivlin
    1962   "Place of residence as a factor in housing desires and
            expectations."   Rural Sociology 27:483-491.

Montgomery, James E., and Gracia S. McCabe
    1973   "Housing aspirations of southern Appalachian fami-
            lies."   Home Economics Research Journal 2:2-11.

Morris, Earl W., and Mary Winter
    1975   "A theory of family housing adjustment."   Journal of
            Marriage and the Family 37:79-88.

Morris, Earl W., and Mary Winter
    1976   "Housing and occupational subcultures." Housing
            Educators Journal 3:2-16.

Morris, Earl W., and Mary Winter
    1978   Housing, Family and Society. New York: Wiley.

Morris, Richard T.
    1956   "A typology of norms." American Sociological Review
            21:610-613.

Morrison, Bonnie Maas, Joanne Goodman Keith, and James J.
Zuiches
    1977   "Energy impacts on Michigan families." Paper pre-
            sented at the annual meeting of the Society for the
            Study of Social Problems, Chicago.

Muessig, Paul
    1979   "Industrialization in housing." Pp. 31-46 in C. S.
            Wedin and L. G. Nygren (eds.), Housing Perspec-
            tives. Minneapolis: Burgess.

National Association of Home Builders
    1981   Housing at the Turning Point. Washington, D.C.:
            National Association of Home Builders.

National Association of Home Builders
    1982   Housing Background. Washington, D.C.: National
            Association of Home Builders.

Newman, Dorothy K., and Dawn Day
    1975   The American Energy Consumer. Cambridge, MA:
            Ballinger.

Newmark, Norma L., and Patricia J. Thompson
    1977   Self, Space and Shelter: An Introduction to Housing.
            San Francisco: Canfield.

New Republic
    1975   "The obsolete home." New Republic 173 (Septem-
            ber 6)):5-8.

Norcross, Carl
    1973   Townhouses and Condominiums: Residents' Likes and
            Dislikes. Washington, D.C.: Urban Land Institute.

Obudho, Robert A.
    1976   "Social indicators for housing and urban development
            in Africa." Social Indicators Research 3:431-449.

Office of Program Planning and Fiscal Management
1976a   Pocket Data Book, 1976.   Olympia, WA: Office of
         Program Planning and Fiscal Management.

Office of Program Planning and Fiscal Management
1976b   State   of   Washington   Population   Trends,   1976.
         Olympia, WA: Office of Program Planning and Fiscal
         Management, Population Studies Division.

Olson, S. C., and D. K. Meredith
1973   Wheelchair Interiors.   Chicago: National Easter Seal
         Society for Crippled Children and Adults.

Packard, Vance
1972   A Nation of Strangers.   New York: McKay.

Parsons, Talcott
1959   "General theory in sociology."   Pp. 3-38 in R. K.
         Merton, L. Brown and L. S. Cottrell, Jr. (eds.),
         Sociology Today.   New York: Basic.

Payne, Judy, and Geoff Payne
1977   "Housing pathways and stratification: A study of life
         chances in the housing market."   Journal of Social
         Policy 6:129-156.

Prescott, James R.
1974   Economic Aspects of Public Housing.   Beverly Hills:
         Sage.

Professional Builder
1975   "Professional builder's national consumer building sur-
         vey on housing."   Professional Builder (Janu-
         ary):81-97.

Reiss, Albert J., Jr.
1963   "Status,   deprivation   and   delinquent   behavior."
         Sociological Quarterly 4:135-150.

Riemer, Svend
1947   "Sociological perspective in home planning."   American
         Sociological Review 12:155-159.

Rodman, Hyman
1963   "The lower class value stretch."   Social Forces 42:
         205-215.

Rojek, Dean G., Frank Clemente, and Gene F. Summers
1975   "Community   satisfaction."   Rural   Sociology   40:
         177-192.

Rosow, Irving
  1948   "Home ownership motives."   American Sociological
         Review 13:751-756.

Rossi, Peter H.
  1955   Why Families Move. Glencoe, IL: Free Press.

Rushing, William A.
  1970   "Class differences in goal orientations and aspira-
         tions: Rural patterns." Rural Sociology 35:377-395.

Saltman, Juliet Z.
  1975   "Implementing open housing laws through social
         action." Journal of Applied Behavioral Science 11:
         39-61.

Schuman, Howard, and Michael P. Johnson
  1976   "Attitudes and behavior." Annual Review of Soci-
         ology 2:161-207.

Schurr, Sam H.
  1971   Energy Research Needs. Washington, D.C.: U.S.
         Department of Commerce, National Technical Informa-
         tion Service.

Select Committee on Nutrition and Human Needs, U.S. Senate
  1971   Promises to Keep, Housing Need and Federal Failure
         in Rural America. Washington, D.C.: U.S. Govern-
         ment Printing Office.

Shils, Edward A.
  1963   "The theory of mass society." Pp. 30-47 in P. Olson
         (ed.), America as a Mass Society. New York: Free
         Press.

Shinn, Allen M., Jr.
  1971   "Measuring the utility of housing: Demonstrating a
         methodological approach." Social Science Quarterly
         52:88-102.

Smith, Ruth H., Donna B. Dower, and Mildred T. Lynch
  1969   "The man in the house." The Family Coordinator
         18:107-111.

Solomon, Arthur P.
  1974   Housing the Urban Poor: A Critical Evaluation of
         Federal Housing Policy. Cambridge, MA: MIT Press.

Sommer, Robert
    1974a "The effect of near environment on people." Forum
           (Fall/Winter):14-15.

Sommer, Robert
    1974b Tight   Spaces: Hard   Architecture   and   How   to
           Humanize It. Englewood Cliffs, NJ: Prentice-Hall.

Sumka, Howard J.
    1977   "Measuring the quality of housing: An econometric
           analysis of tax appraisal records." Land Economics
           53:298-309.

Summer, William Graham
    1906   Folkways. Boston: Ginn.

Taggart, Robert III
    1970   Low Income Housing: A Critique of Aid.   Baltimore,
           MD: Johns Hopkins University Press.

Tallman, Irving, and Romona Morgner
    1970   "Life-style differences among urban and suburban
           blue-collar families." Social Forces 48:334-348.

Thornburg, Kathy R.
    1975   "Apartment environments and socialization of young
           children."   Home   Economics   Research   Journal
           3:192-197.

Time
    1973   "Land use: The rage for reform." Time (Octo-
           ber 1): 94-98.

Tremblay, Kenneth R., Jr., and Riley E. Dunlap
    1978   "Rural-urban residence and concern with environ-
           mental quality." Rural Sociology 43:474-491.

Tremblay, Kenneth R., Jr., Joye J. Dillman, and Don A.
Dillman
    1978   Toward a Sociology of Housing: A Working Biblio-
           graphy.   Monticello, IL: Council of Planning
           Librarians, Exchange Bibliography 1485.

U.S. Bureau of the Census
    1972a 1970 Census of Population: General Social and Eco-
           nomic Characteristics.   Washington, D.C.:   U.S.
           Government Printing Office.

U.S. Bureau of the Census
1972b Housing Characteristics for States, Cities, and Counties. Washington, D.C.: U.S. Government Printing Office.

U.S. Bureau of the Census
1976 Statistical Abstract of the United States. Washington, D.C.: U.S. Government Printing Office.

U.S. Bureau of the Census
1978 Current Housing Reports: General Housing Characteristics for the United States and Regions: 1976, Part A. Washington, D.C.: U.S. Government Printing Office.

U.S. Bureau of the Census
1979 Annual Housing Survey: 1977. General Housing Characteristics, Part A. Washington, D.C.: U.S. Government Printing Office.

U.S. Bureau of the Census
1980 New One-Family Houses Sold and For Sale. Construction Report C25-80-8. Washington, D.C.: U.S. Government Printing Office.

U.S. News and World Report
1979a "Houses in the '80s: Smaller, fewer, costlier." U.S. News and World Report 86 (April 2):54-56.

U.S. News and World Report
1979b "How tax loopholes widen U.S. deficit." U.S. News and World Report 86 (June 18):63-64.

U.S. News and World Report
1980 "Homes--America's unaffordable dream." U.S. News and World Report 88 (June 16):12.

U.S. News and World Report
1983 "Tax subsidies: They just keep climbing." U.S. News and World Report 94 (March 21):75.

Wedin, Carol S.
1979 "A historical perspective of major forms in American housing." Pp. 17-27 in C. S. Wedin and L. G. Nygren (eds.), Housing Perspectives. Minneapolis: Burgess.

Welfeld, Irving H.
1977 "American housing policy: Perverse programs by prudent people." The Public Interest 48:128-144.

Williams, J. Allen, Jr.
    1971   "The multifamily housing solution and housing type
            preferences."   Social Science Quarterly 52:543-559.

Williams, Robin
    1959   American Society.   New York: Knopf.

Williams, Roger M.
    1978   "The assault on fortress suburbia."   Saturday Review
            (Feb. 18):17-22.

Wilson, James Q. (ed.)
    1967   Urban Renewal: The Record and the Controversy.
            Cambridge, MA: MIT Press.

Winter, Mary, and Earl W. Morris
    1976   A Reporting Error Model of Class Variations in Hous-
            ing Norms.   Ames, IA: Home Economics Experiment
            Station, Iowa State University.

Winter, Mary, and Earl W. Morris
    1977   "The housing we would like."   Journal of Home Eco-
            nomics 69:7-10.

Wirth, Louis
    1947   "Housing as a field of sociological research."   Ameri-
            can Sociological Review 12:137-143.

Yearns, Mary H.
    1979   "Government housing programs."   Pp. 83-92 in C. S.
            Wedin and L. G. Nygren (eds.), Housing Perspec-
            tives.   Minneapolis: Burgess.

Zey-Ferrell, Mary, Eleanor A. Kelley, and Alvin L. Bertrand
    1977   "Consumer preferences and selected socioeconomic
            variables related to physical adequacy of housing."
            Home Economics Research Journal 5:232-243.

Appendix A

YOUR HOME

Does It Meet
Your Needs ?

Apartment? Townhouse? Duplex? Single family house? Mobile Home? Other?

A STATEWIDE SURVEY OF WASHINGTON
RESIDENTS: PROBLEMS WITH PRESENT
HOUSING AND HOPES FOR THE FUTURE

If you are married or share your home with another adult, then either of you may complete the questionnaire. But, we would like for the one who does not complete the questionnaire to give us their opinions on the unattached "extra page" which is enclosed.

If you are the only adult in your home, then please fill out the questionnaire and leave the "extra page" blank.

This is the first statewide study of its kind ever done, and we really appreciate your help! Many thanks!

The Home Economics Research Center and the Department of Rural Sociology
Washington State University, Pullman, Washington 99164

Q-1 We would like to begin by asking you to describe the home in which you
     now live. Which one of the following pictures comes closest to describ-
     ing your present home? (Circle number of your answer)

     1 APARTMENT BUILDING   2 TOWN HOUSE (SHARED   3 DUPLEX
                                  SIDEWALLS)

     4 MOBILE HOME (SINGLE   5 MOBILE HOME WITH   6 APARTMENT IN
        OR DOUBLE WIDE)   ATTACHED STRUCTURE   A HOUSE

     7 A SINGLE FAMILY HOUSE   8 None of these pictures seem to fit. Please
                                    describe in this space.

Q-2 How many years have you lived in this home?

                    _____NUMBER OF YEARS
                            (If less than one year put number
                             of months here_____)

Q-3 To the best of your knowledge, about when was your home built? We mean first
     constructed and not when remodeled, added to, or converted. (Circle number
     of your answer)

                    1 1975 OR AFTER
                    2 1970 TO 1974
                    3 1960 TO 1969
                    4 1950 TO 1959
                    5 1940 TO 1949
                    6 BEFORE 1940

Q-4 Which one of the following best describes the condition of your home?

                    1 EXCELLENT CONDITION
                    2 GOOD CONDITION, NEEDS SOME MINOR REPAIRS
                    3 ADEQUATE CONDITION, NEEDS MANY REPAIRS BUT MOSTLY MINOR ONES
                    4 POOR CONDITION, NEEDS SOME MAJOR REPAIRS
                    5 VERY POOR CONDITION, NEEDS TO BE TORN DOWN

-2-

Q-5 How many different rooms of each kind listed below are in your home? Please do not count any space in an unfinished basement or any part of your home that is rented out to members of another household. (Put number in blank: If none put "0")

_____BEDROOM

_____BATHROOM (How many of these are complete; that is have flush toilet, washbasin with piped water and bathtub or shower?_____)

_____LIVING ROOM (If this includes a dining area check here_____)

_____KITCHEN (If this includes a dining area check here_____)

_____SEPARATE DINING ROOM

_____FAMILY OR RECREATION ROOM

_____DEN OR STUDY

_____UTILITY OR LAUNDRY ROOM

_____WORKSHOP OR HOBBY ROOM

OTHER (Please list)

_____ _____

_____ _____

Q-6 Here are some characteristics which your home might have. Please circle the number of all those which you have:

1 FIREPLACE (If yes, how many?_____)

2 GARAGE (If yes, how many parking stalls?_____)

3 CARPORT (If yes, how many parking stalls?_____)

4 UNFINISHED BASEMENT

5 ATTIC

6 DECK OR PORCH

7 PATIO

8 SWIMMING POOL

9 CENTRAL AIR CONDITIONER

10 ROOM AIR CONDITIONER (If yes, how many rooms is it used for?_____)

11 NONE OF THESE

Q-7 About how many square feet of floor space do you have in your home? Do not include a garage that happens to be a part of your house, an unfinished basement, or any part of your home that is rented out to members of another household.

1 LESS THAN 500 SQUARE FEET
2 501 - 1000 SQUARE FEET
3 1001 - 2000 SQUARE FEET
4 2001 - 3000 SQUARE FEET
5 MORE THAN 3000 SQUARE FEET

The way to find square feet is to multiply length X width.

For example, this one story house has 800 square feet.

If your house has more than one story add the square feet for each story.

40 feet

20 feet

20 X 40 = 800 SQUARE FEET

Q-8 One of the most talked about housing concerns these days is <u>costs</u>. On these pages we would like for you to explain as best you can the costs of living in your home, and how you feel about what you are getting for your money.

IF YOU RENT
Please answer these questions

8-A <u>About</u> how much a <u>month</u> do you pay for rent? (Circle number of your answer)

    1 LESS THAN $50
    2 $50 TO $99
    3 $100 TO $149
    4 $150 TO $199
    5 $200 TO $249
    6 $250 TO $299
    7 $300 OR MORE

8-B On the <u>average</u> about how much per <u>month</u> do you pay for these items? (If nothing put "0," if included in the rent put "R")

$_____ELECTRICITY

$_____GAS, OIL, OR COAL

$_____WATER

$_____GARBAGE

$_____OTHER (Please specify)

_____

8-C Altogether how many separate households (apartments or units) are located in the building where you live?

    1 ONE (only yours)
    2 TWO
    3 THREE TO FIVE
    4 SIX TO NINE
    5 10 OR MORE

8-D How good of a job does your landlord do in taking care of your home?

    1 POOR
    2 FAIR
    3 GOOD
    4 EXCELLENT

IF YOU OWN (Including mobile home owners who rent their space)
Please answer these questions

8-A What is the value of your home? That is <u>about</u> how much do you think it would <u>sell</u> for if it were for sale? (If your home is part of a farm or other business see note at bottom of page)

    1 LESS THAN $10,000
    2 $10,000 TO $19,999
    3 $20,000 TO $29,999
    4 $30,000 TO $39,999
    5 $40,000 TO $49,999
    6 $50,000 TO $75,000
    7 MORE THAN $75,000

8-B On the <u>average</u> about how much per month do you pay for these items? (If none put "0")

$_____LOAN PAYMENTS

$_____ELECTRICITY

$_____GAS, OIL, OR COAL

$_____WATER

$_____GARBAGE

$_____PROPERTY TAXES

$_____SPACE RENT (For mobile homes only)

$_____OTHER (Please specify)

_____

8-C Is any part of your home rented out to others?

    1 NO
    2 YES

8-D (If yes) How many separate apartments do you rent to others?

    _____NUMBER

NOTE: If your home is on 10 acres or more, or any part of your property is used as a commercial establishment or medical office, check here ▢ and answer the questions as best you can for the residential part of your property.

⎛ EVERYONE--Please answer these questions ⎞

Q-9 How do your housing costs compare to what you feel you can afford to pay for
     housing? Are the costs you just listed more or less than you feel you can
     afford to pay? (Circle number of your answer)

                    1 MUCH MORE THAN YOU CAN AFFORD
                    2 A LITTLE MORE THAN YOU CAN AFFORD
                    3 ABOUT WHAT YOU CAN AFFORD
                    4 A LITTLE LESS THAN YOU CAN AFFORD
                    5 MUCH LESS THAN YOU CAN AFFORD

Q-10 If you were free to choose between renting or owning a home, would you:

                    1 VERY STRONGLY PREFER TO RENT
                    2 STRONGLY PREFER TO RENT
                    3 SOMEWHAT PREFER TO RENT
                    4 NO PREFERENCE
                    5 SOMEWHAT PREFER TO OWN
                    6 STRONGLY PREFER TO OWN
                    7 VERY STRONGLY PREFER TO OWN

Q-11 Which best describes where your home is located?

                    1 A LOT INSIDE THE CITY LIMITS
                    2 A MOBILE HOME PARK
                    3 A PLACE IN COUNTRY, LESS THAN
                       10 ACRES
                    4 A PLACE IN COUNTRY, MORE THAN
                       10 ACRES
                    5 OTHER (Please specify)
                    _____

Q-12 Which best describes the lot on which your home is located:

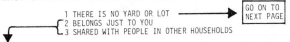

                    1 THERE IS NO YARD OR LOT ──────────▶ ┌─────────────┐
                                                           │ GO ON TO   │
                    2 BELONGS JUST TO YOU   │ NEXT PAGE   │
                    3 SHARED WITH PEOPLE IN OTHER HOUSEHOLDS└─────────────┘

Q-13 Does this yard or lot have: (Circle all that apply)

                    1 A LAWN
                    2 SOME TREES AND SHRUBS
                    3 SOME FLOWERS
                    4 A VEGETABLE GARDEN
                    5 A FENCE AROUND SOME OR ALL OF IT
                    6 NONE OF THESE

Q-14 On the average how much time a week do the members of your household spend
     during the summer months caring for any trees, flowers, lawn, and garden?

                    1 NONE
                    2 1-5 HOURS
                    3 6-10 HOURS
                    4 11-20 HOURS
                    5 MORE THAN 20 HOURS PER WEEK

Q-15 Many people have been kind enough to tell us what they like and do not like
      about their present home. Here are some of the complaints they have mentioned.
      Please indicate whether each one is NOT a complaint, a SLIGHT complaint, a
      MODERATE complaint or a BIG complaint you have about your present home.

Possible Complaints	To what extent is this a complaint? (Please circle your answer)		
1 Yard (or lot) is too small...................NOT	SLIGHT	MODERATE	BIG
2 No fireplace................................NOT	SLIGHT	MODERATE	BIG
3 Poorly constructed..........................NOT	SLIGHT	MODERATE	BIG
4 Too small: not enough space inside..........NOT	SLIGHT	MODERATE	BIG
5 Not a very nice neighborhood.................NOT	SLIGHT	MODERATE	BIG
6 Outside appearance is not very nice..........NOT	SLIGHT	MODERATE	BIG
7 Home is not as nice as those of our friends..NOT	SLIGHT	MODERATE	BIG
8 Costs too much to live in it.................NOT	SLIGHT	MODERATE	BIG
9 Badly needs some repairs.....................NOT	SLIGHT	MODERATE	BIG
10 Not a very comfortable or relaxing place in which to live............................NOT	SLIGHT	MODERATE	BIG
11 Not enough rooms............................NOT	SLIGHT	MODERATE	BIG
12 Room arrangement does not provide adequate privacy from other members of household....NOT	SLIGHT	MODERATE	BIG
13 A lack of privacy from neighbors............NOT	SLIGHT	MODERATE	BIG
14 Neighborhood is too noisy...................NOT	SLIGHT	MODERATE	BIG
15 Too far from schools or other community services...................................NOT	SLIGHT	MODERATE	BIG
16 Yard (or lot) is too big....................NOT	SLIGHT	MODERATE	BIG
17 Inside is dull and uninteresting............NOT	SLIGHT	MODERATE	BIG
18 Too big: too much space inside.............NOT	SLIGHT	MODERATE	BIG
19 I do not feel very safe in it...............NOT	SLIGHT	MODERATE	BIG
20 Is poorly insulated.........................NOT	SLIGHT	MODERATE	BIG
21 Requires too much work to care for it.......NOT	SLIGHT	MODERATE	BIG
22 Not a very good place to entertain friends...NOT	SLIGHT	MODERATE	BIG
23 Rooms poorly arranged so that activities of one person interfere with others...........NOT	SLIGHT	MODERATE	BIG
24 Any other complaints (Please list)			
_____NOT	SLIGHT	MODERATE	BIG
_____NOT	SLIGHT	MODERATE	BIG
_____NOT	SLIGHT	MODERATE	BIG

Q-16 Overall, how satisfied are you with your present housing situation?

> 1 EXTREMELY DISSATISFIED
> 2 QUITE DISSATISFIED
> 3 SOMEWHAT DISSATISFIED
> 4 NEITHER SATISFIED OR DISSATISFIED
> 5 SOMEWHAT SATISFIED
> 6 QUITE SATISFIED
> 7 EXTREMELY SATISFIED

Q-17 Now, please take a minute and look at these "ladders." Suppose the top step
(#10) represents the best possible housing in which you could hope to live,
and the bottom step (#0) represents the worst, then . . .

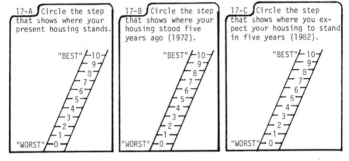

17-A Circle the step that shows where your present housing stands.

17-B Circle the step that shows where your housing stood five years ago (1972).

17-C Circle the step that shows where you expect your housing to stand in five years (1982).

Q-18 Which of the following best describes how you would feel about moving out of
your present home into a "better" housing situation?

> 1 NO DESIRE TO MOVE
> 2 ONLY A SLIGHT DESIRE TO MOVE
> 3 A DEFINITE DESIRE TO MOVE
> 4 A VERY STRONG DESIRE TO MOVE

Q-19 During the past year have you tried to find better housing?

> 1 NO, I HAVE NOT TRIED
> 2 TRIED, BUT NOT VERY HARD
> 3 TRIED MODERATELY HARD
> 4 TRIED VERY HARD

Q-20 How likely do you think it is that you will move into a home that better suits
your housing desires in the next five years?

> 1 VERY UNLIKELY
> 2 SOMEWHAT UNLIKELY
> 3 DO NOT KNOW
> 4 SOMEWHAT LIKELY
> 5 VERY LIKELY

Q-21 Just suppose that for some reason you had to move out of your present home and you were given a chance to live in each of the places listed below during the <u>next five years</u>. To what extent would you <u>consider</u> each choice?

Choices	Would you consider this choice? (Circle your answer)				
	DEFINITELY NO	PROBABLY NO	UNSURE	PROBABLY YES	DEFINITELY YES
1 Buy a mobile home located in a rented space in a mobile home park.........................DEF-NO		P-NO	UNSURE	P-YES	DEF-YES
2 Buy a mobile home located on a lot that you also buy.............DEF-NO		P-NO	UNSURE	P-YES	DEF-YES
3 Buy a single family house.........DEF-NO		P-NO	UNSURE	P-YES	DEF-YES
4 Buy a townhouse (shares side wall with houses next door).......DEF-NO		P-NO	UNSURE	P-YES	DEF-YES
5 Rent a single family house........DEF-NO		P-NO	UNSURE	P-YES	DEF-YES
6 Rent an apartment in a building containing 5 or more other apartments......................DEF-NO		P-NO	UNSURE	P-YES	DEF-YES
7 Rent a unit in a duplex...........DEF-NO		P-NO	UNSURE	P-YES	DEF-YES

Q-22 Which of the above would you most prefer to live in? (Put number of choice in box)

☐ MOST PREFER   ☐ SECOND MOST PREFER

Q-23 Which one of the above would you most dislike? (Put number of choice in box)

☐ MOST DISLIKE   ☐ SECOND MOST DISLIKE

Q-24 Suppose you could live in your "most preferred" home in any location you liked. Which size of <u>county</u> would you most prefer? (Circle number of your answer)

    1 LARGE METROPOLITAN COUNTY: CONTAINS CITY OF 150,000 OR MORE PEOPLE, SEVERAL SUBURBS, SMALLER TOWNS, AND ONLY A LITTLE OPEN COUNTRY
    2 SMALL METROPOLITAN COUNTY: CITY OF 50,000 TO 149,999 PEOPLE, SMALLER TOWNS, AND SOME OPEN COUNTRY
    3 SMALL URBAN COUNTY: CONTAINS CITY OF 10,000 TO 49,999 PEOPLE, A FEW SMALLER TOWNS, AND CONSIDERABLE OPEN COUNTRY
    4 RURAL COUNTY: CONTAINS CITY OF LESS THAN 10,000 PEOPLE, A FEW SMALLER TOWNS, AND MOSTLY OPEN COUNTRY

Q-25 Where would you want your home located within the <u>county</u> you just chose? (Circle number of your answer)

    1 NEAR DOWNTOWN AREA OF THE COUNTY'S LARGEST CITY
    2 AWAY FROM DOWNTOWN AREA IN THE COUNTY'S LARGEST CITY
    3 IN ONE OF THE COUNTY'S SMALLER TOWNS (OR SUBURBS)
    4 IN OPEN COUNTRY LESS THAN 15 MINUTES DRIVE AWAY FROM COUNTY'S LARGEST CITY
    5 IN OPEN COUNTRY MORE THAN 15 MINUTES DRIVE AWAY FROM THE COUNTY'S LARGEST CITY

-8-

Q-26 Several suggestions have been made about how to reduce the amount of <u>energy</u> we use in our homes. We would like to know the extent to which you personally would be able to accept these proposed policies.

WAYS TO DECREASE USE OF ENERGY	VERY HARD TO ACCEPT	SOMEWHAT HARD TO ACCEPT	DON'T KNOW	SOMEWHAT EASY TO ACCEPT	VERY EASY TO ACCEPT
1 Build smaller home 1-2 less rooms than present average	V-HARD	S-HARD	D.K.	S-EASY	V-EASY
2 Build homes partly underground, so only one side has windows	V-HARD	S-HARD	D.K.	S-EASY	V-EASY
3 Allow heat no higher than 65° in winter months	V-HARD	S-HARD	D.K.	S-EASY	V-EASY
4 Allow air conditioning to cool no lower than 85° in summer	V-HARD	S-HARD	D.K.	S-EASY	V-EASY
5 Close off 2-3 rooms of your home and only heat them to 50° in the winter	V-HARD	S-HARD	D.K.	S-EASY	V-EASY
6 Reduce size and number of windows below present average	V-HARD	S-HARD	D.K.	S-EASY	V-EASY
7 Build homes on smaller lots so that the side walls are shared with homes next door	V-HARD	S-HARD	D.K.	S-EASY	V-EASY
8 Stop the building of homes in countryside to cut down energy for transportation to and from work	V-HARD	S-HARD	D.K.	S-EASY	V-EASY
9 Mandatory installation of heavy insulation in existing homes	V-HARD	S-HARD	D.K.	S-EASY	V-EASY

How hard for you to accept? (Circle your answer)

Q-27 If it were necessary to do <u>one</u> of the following in order to conserve energy, which would you be most willing to accept?

    1 BUILD SMALLER HOMES (1-2 less rooms) AND HEAT 1-2 LESS ROOMS IN EXISTING HOMES

    2 STRICTLY LIMIT TEMPERATURE; HEAT TO MAXIMUM 65° IN WINTER; COOL TO MINIMUM 85° IN SUMMER

Q-28 If it were necessary to do one of the following in order to <u>hold down costs</u> of new homes, which would you be most willing to accept?

    1 BUILD SMALLER HOMES (1-2 less rooms) ON AVERAGE SIZE LOTS

    2 BUILD PRESENT SIZE OF HOME ON SMALLER LOT

Finally we would like to ask some questions about yourself for the statistical analysis.

Q-29 In what Washington county is your home located?

_____COUNTY

Q-30 What town or city do you depend on most for goods and services?

_____TOWN OR CITY

Q-31 In general how satisfied are you with the community in which you live?

1 EXTREMELY DISSATISFIED
2 QUITE DISSATISFIED
3 SOMEWHAT DISSATISFIED
4 NEITHER SATISFIED OR DISSATISFIED
5 SOMEWHAT SATISFIED
6 QUITE SATISFIED
7 EXTREMELY SATISFIED

Q-32 Are you:

1 MARRIED
2 DIVORCED
3 WIDOWED
4 SEPARATED
5 SINGLE

Q-33 Since a big part of this study concerns your feelings about the home in which you presently live, it is very important for us to know who lives in your household. Please list everyone, starting with yourself.

Who? (e.g., wife, husband, son, daughter, parent, friend)	Age (in years)	Sex (M=male F=female)
1 _Yourself_	☐	☐
2 _____	☐	☐
3 _____	☐	☐
4 _____	☐	☐
5 _____	☐	☐
6 _____	☐	☐
7 _____	☐	☐

Q-34 Do you (or your spouse) have any children in addition to any mentioned above?

1 NO
2 YES   (if yes) How many under 18?_____
                   How many over 18?_____

Q-35 Within the next five years do you expect the number of people living in your home to most likely increase, decrease, or stay the same?

1 TO INCREASE
2 STAY THE SAME
3 TO DECREASE

-10-

Please answer these questions for yourself <u>and</u> your spouse or living partner if you have one.

YOURSELF	YOUR SPOUSE or LIVING PARTNER
Q-36 Are you: (Circle number of answer)	Is this person: (Circle number of answer)

1 EMPLOYED FULL TIME	1 EMPLOYED FULL TIME
2 EMPLOYED PART TIME	2 EMPLOYED PART TIME
3 UNEMPLOYED	3 UNEMPLOYED
4 FULL TIME HOMEMAKER	4 FULL TIME HOMEMAKER
5 RETIRED	5 RETIRED

. . . .

Q-37 <u>Your</u> usual occupation:	<u>Their</u> usual occupation:

_____TITLE   _____TITLE

_____KIND OF WORK   _____KIND OF WORK

_____COMPANY OR   _____COMPANY OR
                 BUSINESS   BUSINESS

. . . .

Q-38 The highest level of education <u>you</u> have completed:	<u>Their</u> highest level of education completed:

1 NO FORMAL EDUCATION	1 NO FORMAL EDUCATION
2 GRADE SCHOOL	2 GRADE SCHOOL
3 SOME HIGH SCHOOL	3 SOME HIGH SCHOOL
4 HIGH SCHOOL GRADUATE	4 HIGH SCHOOL GRADUATE
5 SOME COLLEGE	5 SOME COLLEGE
6 COLLEGE GRADUATE	6 COLLEGE GRADUATE
7 SOME GRADUATE WORK	7 SOME GRADUATE WORK
8 A GRADUATE DEGREE	8 A GRADUATE DEGREE

. . . .

Q-39 Where <u>you</u> lived most of your life before adulthood:	Where <u>they</u> lived most of their life before adulthood:

1 SMALL TOWN LESS THAN 2,500	1 SMALL TOWN LESS THAN 2,500
2 TOWN 2,500 TO 9,999	2 TOWN 2,500 TO 9,999
3 CITY 10,000 TO 49,999	3 CITY 10,000 TO 49,999
4 CITY 50,000 TO 149,999	4 CITY 50,000 TO 149,999
5 CITY 150,000 OR MORE	5 CITY 150,000 OR MORE

. . . .

Q-40 Before adulthood did <u>you</u> live mostly:	Before adulthood did <u>they</u> live mostly:

1 ON A FARM	1 ON A FARM
2 IN COUNTRYSIDE	2 IN COUNTRYSIDE
3 IN TOWN OR CITY	3 IN TOWN OR CITY

. . . .

Q-41 Finally, which of these broad categories describes your total family income before taxes, in 1976.

1 LESS THAN $5,000	5 $20,000 TO $24,999
2 $5,000 TO $9,999	6 $25,000 TO $34,999
3 $10,000 TO $14,999	7 $35,000 TO $49,999
4 $15,000 TO $19,999	8 $50,000 OR MORE

Is there anything else you would like to tell us about your present home or the kind of home in which you would like most to live? If so, please use this space for that purpose.

Also, any comments you wish to make that you think may help us in future efforts to understand what Washington residents want from their homes will be appreciated, either here or in a separate letter.

Your contribution to this effort is very greatly appreciated.

If you would like a summary of results, please print your name and

address on the back of the return envelope (NOT on this questionnaire).

We will see that you get it.

Appendix B

OTHER PUBLICATIONS

This book is one of several publications resulting from research conducted under Agricultural Research Center Project 0377, a joint project of the Home Economics Research Center and Department of Rural Sociology at Washington State University, Pullman, Washington 99164. Other publications from this project are listed here:

Dillman, Joye J., Kenneth R. Tremblay, Jr., and Don A. Dillman
1977   "Energy policies directed at the home: Which ones will people accept?" Housing Educators Journal 4: 2-13.

Tremblay, Kenneth R., Jr., Don A. Dillman, and Joye J. Dillman
1977   Housing Satisfactions and Preferences of Washington Residents: A 1977 Statewide Survey. Pullman, WA: College of Agriculture Research Center, Washington State University, Circular 605.

Tremblay, Kenneth R., Jr., Joye J. Dillman, and Don A. Dillman
1978   Toward a Sociology of Housing: A Working Bibliography. Monticello, IL: Council of Planning Librarians, Exchange Bibliography 1485.

Dillman, Don A.
1979   "Residential preferences, quality of life and the population turnaround." American Journal of Agricultural Economics 61 (5):960-966.

Dillman, Don A., Kenneth R. Tremblay, Jr., and Joye J. Dillman
1979   "Influence of housing norms and personal characteristics on stated housing preferences." Housing and Society 6:2-19.

Tremblay, Kenneth R., Jr., Don A. Dillman, and Kent D. Van Liere
1980   "An examination of the relationship between housing preferences and community-size preferences." Rural Sociology 45:509-519.

Tremblay, Kenneth R., Jr., Don A. Dillman, and Joye J. Dillman
    1981   "Acceptable housing alternatives." HUD Challenge 12 (January):25-27.

Dillman, Don A., Kenneth R. Tremblay, Jr., and Joye J. Dillman
    1982   "Mobile homes: Should small town policies change?" Small Town 12:18-22.

Dillman, Don A., Joye J. Dillman, and Michael L. Schwalbe
    1982   "Strength of housing norms and willingness to accept housing alternatives," Housing and Society (Special Issue: Proceedings of the 1980 Annual Conference):123-132.

Index

About the Authors

Kenneth R. Tremblay, Jr., is Assistant Professor of Housing, Department of Home Economics, University of Arkansas, Fayetteville. He received his Ph.D. in sociology from Washington State University, and has taught previously at the University of South Dakota and the University of Nebraska. Major publications include articles in Housing and Society, Rural Sociology, Policy Studies Journal, Housing Science, and Small Town, as well as an edited book on residential energy conservation. His major interests lie in the social aspects of housing, especially housing preferences and norms.

Don A. Dillman is Professor, Department of Sociology, and Research and Extension Sociologist, Department of Rural Sociology at Washington State University. He received his Ph.D. in sociology from Iowa State University. A National Kellogg Fellow, 1980-83, he is currently president of the (North American) Rural Sociology Society. His publications include two books, Mail and Telephone Surveys: The Total Design Method and Rural Society in the U.S.: Issues for the 1980s, as well as many journal articles. Current academic interests in addition to the sociology of housing include survey methods, the diffusion of innovations, and social aspects of the information society.